DANDELION

A warrior beside him

Dear Jenn,

May the words of this book
encourage and inspire your own
Ezer Kenegdo journey.

With much Love,
Honna

John 3:30
Gen 2:18

TABLE OF CONTENTS

Photo taken by Steve Taylor | 2006 | Masai Mara, Kenya

ezer kenedgo

A-zar kin-egg-DOE

The first letter "e" is pronounced as a long "A" sound.
Emphasis/accent in the first word is on the first syllable.
Emphasis/accent in the second word is on the last syllable.

FOREWORD

by Steve Taylor

The book you are holding was written with the heartfelt intention of introducing a new way of looking at marriage. Can any more ways of being better at this age-old institution be introduced to help couples on their life journeys together? Haven't all these areas been explored? Is this like another weight-loss program that doesn't actually work? Well, maybe it works for a little while and then we fall back into old neuron paths of destruction only to end up where we began or maybe even a little worse. Since God created man and woman, when Adam and Eve became husband and wife, the enemy of our Lord has been hammering married couples in an attempt to destroy everything God had intended for good. His perfect design for a man and a woman to live harmoniously, to work together to provide for their home, raise children if they are so blessed, to be encouragers to each other—all for the purpose of representing the relationship of Christ and the church (Ephesians

5:25). When God created man, he could see Adam needed help. Because Adam was incompetent and couldn't make it on his own? No. But a life spent alone would not produce the potential God designed for man and woman.

So what are we talking about here? The Bible says God made a helper suitable for him (Genesis 2:18). The world has been stuck on the word "helper" ever since. The English meaning for this word is translated as an assistant, a worker, a subordinate, someone in lower standing who is to do what he or she is told to do. You know what I mean. You see it in homes all over the world and it isn't working so well, is it? You probably know of a home like this. You may have the same struggles.

In the Bible, Genesis was written in Hebrew, and we find that the word for helper was "ezer." What is an ezer? Wait. Before we look at that, let's go over it again while my male brain sorts through this the way it has been played out for centuries.

God created the man.
He saw that the man needed help.
So he made a woman to fill that role.

Man was first: he led.
Woman was made second.
She's the helper.

The leader tells the helper what to do, when to do it, how to do it, and how many times to do it, right? (And I'm not talking about sex.) I'm talking about everything in the marriage.

But before we go too far... the word *"ezer"* is used a few more times throughout the Bible, but most of those times it speaks of God himself as the *ezer*—the helper. Are we in a position to tell God what to do?

No, and when we do try to tell God what to do, it doesn't go so well. With that in mind, the word *ezer* was intended to mean helper, but more. It is also described as being a defender and a protector.

Another Hebrew word was used to complete this God-given title for women that describes her as being "similar to" him—beside him, like a partner in life. The word is *kenegdo*. The basic combination of the two—*ezer kenegdo*—reveals that the woman, the wife, is to be a helper and a protector beside her husband, someone to watch his back and to keep him from making unwise choices that the devil himself is more than happy to accommodate.

We will also tell you that the translation of these words has changed over the years and there are many biblical scholars who may be quick to correct what this book is all about, but our goal is for you to see that when we realize God's full intentions for husbands and wives, the blessings of marriage flow.

When I look at my wife, I see a woman who loves God deeply. A woman who pursues truth and all that is good. I know no one who prays more, reads more, gives more, serves more, and makes continual sacrifices for the sake of others, all to bring glory to God and not herself.

She pays close attention to details I am oblivious to in order to make things better for everyone around her, starting with me. She has been and still is willing to fight for me, even with me, to reveal the harmful things that I don't see. My Pa Thomas told me, "Find a woman who will help you in this life." I did. He knew what an *ezer* was even though he didn't speak Hebrew or had he ever heard the word. But he knew because he had an *ezer* who helped him be more than he could possibly be on his own. This is knowledge I have passed on to our sons and to many young men who were hoping to find the "one" to journey through life with. My *ezer* has been practicing this for 34 years, because she knows it's important to her Lord. If it's important to him, it's a priority for her. I haven't always made it easy for her to do her job, but she has been diligent to see the things I cannot.

We have been serving as missionaries in Kenya for several years teaching about marriage and family to pastors and counselors. When we first arrived, so did the deceiver. He was determined to cut us in two and stop what God had sent us to share with the people of this African culture. Here's where I confess that for the majority of my life, I had been unknowingly allowing sin into our home. Selfishness, pride, stubbornness, laziness, procrastination, and passive-aggressive behaviors can be bold or they can be subtle, and I was leaving the door wide open for them to walk in and destroy us. I couldn't see it, but my God-given *ezer* could. And God had had enough. So he brought me to the end of myself, so that I could finally see the gift my wife had been all along. She persevered out of obedience to the promise she made to God and to me. Remember the vows "for better or worse"? A true *ezer* will do that... if you let her. God's plan really works.

This ancient "new" word "*ezer*" has been overlooked for years, but why? Is it because it will take away the high-held positions of men who would rather rule over their wives than have them stand beside them? We live in a selfish world where people take advantage of the "weaker" for their own benefit. What's happening is tragic and reaping deserved results due to lack of obedience and respect. Galatians 6:7 tells us, "Do not be deceived: God cannot be mocked. A man reaps what he sows."

Are you beginning to see that our Creator's plans were to give us abundant lives, which included the husband/wife relationship? To bring the strengths we possess together for the glory of God and to die to self so that his light will shine on an unknowing world. We need only to follow his rules. Isaiah 48:17–18 tells us, "I am the Lord your God, who teaches you what is best for you, who directs you in the way you should go. If you had only paid attention to my commands, your peace would have been like a river." Who doesn't want a river of peace to flow into his or her life? So take this time to listen to the benefits that have been provided through God's promises. You are about to learn from a good teacher who will warmly help you understand more—the more that has the potential to change your marriage relationship, that can help free you from the binding lies that have robbed you and your spouse of the "all" that was intended.

Meet my *ezer*. Her name is Donna. Some call her Mom. Some call her daughter-in-love. Some in Kenya call her Mama Mandazi. Some call her Shosho. I call her Beauty, the best *ezer* I know.

A Note from the Author

If given a chance, most little girls would grow up wondering about the possibility of becoming the princess who is rescued by the knight in shining armor. Even if she doesn't need to be rescued, she still dreams of the handsome prince riding in to carry her away to live happily ever after in his castle. Somehow it is a silent hope found in little girls' dreams all over the world. First world to third world, it makes no difference.

But the Scripture is clear, "When I was a child, I talked like a child, I thought like a child, I reasoned like a child. When I became a [wo]man, I put the ways of childhood behind me" (1 Corinthians 13:11). These are easy words to read, more challenging to actually live. We can get caught up in thinking like a child even though we look nothing like one in our grown-up world. So many women I know are caring for hearth and home, raising children, and managing successful careers, but at their cores, they're still dreaming their secret childhood dreams. When will that prince arrive? Where is the castle I had hoped would be my home? Instead, we're in other places, wondering if maybe we should have turned right when we opted to go left.

This book is my heart on paper for all my princess sisters and for the knights trying to figure out how to mount their horses wearing all that shiny armor. Life has very few castles filled with "living-happily-ever-after" people. Instead, homes are filled with real people working hard. We hope for the best and work to achieve what is needed, but challenges come, and too often we wonder who we are, what we're doing, and why the "happily-ever-after" part never settles in completely. That's been my story, as embarrassing as it is to admit. I've been a Cinderella pretender or a Snow White wannabe wondering when all the little cuddly animals will arrive and start helping me with my household chores—cleaning, cooking, laundry.

Over the last twenty years, God has been whispering to my heart and opening my eyes to the ways HE would describe and define his princess daughters. Walt Disney gave names to his. But it just might be that Walt got the idea of naming his princess characters from the One who created the idea of princesses. For, in truth, every king calls his daughters his princesses. So it is with the King of Kings. He too gave a name to his first daughter—and therein lies the purpose for the book you are holding.

This book wasn't my idea. I've felt unable to write it from the moment it first appeared in my heart. I've asked God to send this message to other women. I've even requested by name the ones I thought he should ask. But after wrestling with God for more than a few years, he has made it clear that it was mine to do in obedience to him. Steve has repeatedly reminded me, "It is yet another way you are worshipping him."

So let me beat you to the punch. I agree with you... someone else could have done a much better job of writing this book. But join me in laying that fact down, and please overlook my imperfections (and there are many). Instead, please allow the importance of the truths on these pages to help you step into "a whole new world" created by the One who made us all. I would not have written this book if he had not guided every word. It is my promise to you.

Before jumping into the book, I want to share two of the innumerable ways God has reassured me about the importance of this sharing. One such reassurance came just a week or two into the initial writing. Talking with our daughter, Maggie (who has graciously and beautifully done all the graphic design and page layouts), she asked me to pray about what simple, universally known image should be used to represent the ezer kenegdo. I was dumbfounded at the request. Completely at a loss, I followed her suggestion and prayed daily.

About a week later, while sitting by the lake at our home in Kenya, I prayed again. Looking down in my quiet meditations, I found a bright, smiling, yellow dandelion looking up at me. I smiled back. Dandelions have always made me smile, but in the last two decades, they've become extra special as our son Peter has made it his mission in life to pluck one for me on almost every walk we've shared. I have a dainty clay pot that holds dried dandelions from the Rocky Mountains in America to Longonot Mountain in Kenya and every space in-between.

As I looked at the silent messenger gleaming its yellow joy up to my questioning mind, it became clear. Dandelions are not planted by anyone—ever. They are considered weeds. No one pays money for them. And yet, they are found in almost every corner of the world. And what do they do? They shine brightly. Even when trampled underfoot or ignored completely, the dandelion continues to bring its simple, joyful message of endurance and strength and hope.

Steve began researching the origin and uses of the dandelion flower-weed. And we were astounded at the countless ways this tiny, often ignored, usually unwanted little glimmer of sunshine shares commonalities with an ezer kenegdo. Hence, as you read, each chapter will share a connection between the name the Father gave his princess daughters with the ever-present flower he sprinkles all over his world.

Donna Taylor

Chapter 1

"The Garden"
What Happened Then Still Happens Now

The dandelion has been blooming for at least 30 million years. This means every person you have ever heard of, read about, or known has walked pathways where this tiny flower lived. It's famous, in an unknown sort of way.

The Shattering...

It was a perfect evening as we peacefully walked through historic streets of an old seaport town. The night air held that wonderful mixture of warm ocean smells and cool coastal breezes. Sea gulls sang overhead, competing with the old-salt crooner outside the corner coffee shop two blocks away. It was one of those rare moments when everyone was kind, no one was in need, the leaves in the trees brushed one another in musical ways, and tears had been given the night off. Even the bench beneath us, with its weathered and worn curves, welcomed us to rest where many others had found solace for countless decades.

Ice cream cones in hand, Steve and I watched as families walked by under twinkling lights strung in ancient oak trees. Peace. Laughter. Joy. Contentment. And then that eerie sound of crackling breakage... the sound that precedes the shattering of a beautiful glass window.

But it was not broken glass that sliced open the picturesque evening. It was her voice, her words. This young woman, likely in her 30s, passed in front of us completely unaware of the joy that gave way in order to accommodate her hasty pace. She turned boldly to her husband, never batting an eye, and said, "Well, if you'd just give me what I want, we wouldn't have any problems." And the street froze. It was only a split second, but for sure the guitarist and the gull held their voices still as the slight glimmer of salty tears began to build in the eyes of the man walking behind her.

The struggle was on.

The man was whipped up one side and down the other, not by leather, but worse, by words. The gleam in her eye boldly declared that she knew she was winning and whatever trinket she fancied was soon to be bagged.

We cringed so acutely, we wondered why neither of them noticed our reactions. It was not as it should have been—for either of them. It was not as it should be in any marriage. But the struggle comes and goes and, in its wake, so many are left wondering, Why even try?

Our guess is that the man gave her what she wanted and for a few hours (or maybe just a few minutes), they appeared to have no problems, just as she had said, "If you'll just give me what I want..." But when the next "I want" rolled around, a new problem would appear, at least until he gave in again. What a painful, sad way to live.

Demand and Supply

A business thrives based on its ability to manage the flow between supply and demand. Fortune 500 companies are perfect examples; they find ways to supply products in high demand, and the rest is history. But in a home, in a marriage, those words too often get flipped into demand and supply. Left unchecked, they become a death sentence for relationships.

Neither the wife nor the husband on the quaint street corner was living the way God intended. They were enduring, struggling, getting their way, or falling in defeat. But the gift of relationship, joy beside each other, companionship with peace... none of these were present. And we winced over the sad looks on both their faces. Getting her way was only a temporary ointment for the something's-not-right feeling she had deep inside her.

It showed in her eyes. And giving her what she wanted in order to keep her "happy" was another mauling of his manliness. He felt it fading away. His broad shoulders and thick wallet made no difference. He knew that she ruled him and he died a little inside.

But what do you do with it even if you're brave enough to admit it? You fight sometimes. You try and stand up for what you think is right. But in the end, the winner wins and somehow you both lose. At other times, you give in quickly and hope that someday it will magically get better and you'll begin to actually enjoy life together... every day... not just when one is getting his or her way.

We can change the setting, recast the main characters, alter the story line just a tad, and BAM, there it is again—hurting couples who maybe started out really liking each other, perhaps even loving each other, but after a few months (or years), one begins getting, the other keeps giving. They struggle over it; get over it; but somehow it seems to grow in the mildewed closets of their hearts. Left unchecked, it brings them to an end... either the end of themselves or the end of their home. Either way, death is sure to come calling even though no one has stopped breathing.

Do We Really Need...?

There's a serious wrong on both their parts and many books on marital conflict and resolutions can help us work through the issues that need to be addressed between wounded couples. But this book is not a book just about marriage; it's a book meant to share a truth that was left behind long ago. Did it get buried in that first garden? It seems it may have.

This book will often refer to relational dynamics in marriage, but it is not a book specifically for marriage. Instead, it focuses predominantly on one-half of the marriage, the wife. What does she really bring to the marriage, the home, the relationship? Even more important is the question: What did God intend her to bring?

She was meant for so much more than we have been able to see as spoken by the One who made her. God's plan for his daughters has been overlooked for so long, some say it is obsolete in today's world. We feel differently. We believe, instead, that understanding those God-breathed words over his girls is perhaps needed more than ever today. Until we understand it, we can't live it. And we can't understand it until someone shares it. So here's to sharing for the hope of authentic understanding, so that heaven's purpose in creating the woman can be lived out in homes unfettered by the tangled weeds that grow in uncared-for gardens.

Let's dig deep into the reasons every wife needs to be seen and heard and cared for, because she has more than we've ever fully realized within her, waiting to be discovered. But if she's not cared for, if she doesn't understand her intended value, her unmet needs may trickle out in wrong ways, ways that end up tearing her home apart rather than holding it together.

Some of you may have flinched at the words "every wife needs," because for centuries, women have been wounded and some have declared that women don't need anything from men. But declaring that wives don't need... well, those are wounded-warrior words. For in truth, we were all made with a heart-shaped need for relationships.

Once Upon a Time, Long, Long Ago...

In the beginning, God created him; God created her; God created them. It was the response to a need that brought about the birth pangs of their creation. And from that day until this, there have been beautiful moments intertwined with moments of hurt. Sometimes the hurt is a shallow scraping, but often it cuts clear to the bone. It was never meant to be this way.

To begin rightly, we should lay a foundation. Let's revisit the garden. After all, it's the historical birthplace of that first woman. Most have heard the story of her creation, but in case you haven't, take a minute to read it for yourself. Her name was Eve and her beginning is found in Genesis 2:18–25. Some of us have heard the story since we were children. But when we hear something many times over, we often begin to think we know it completely. Today, let's take a long, indubitable look at the garden again and see the deeper truths that have for ages been lost somewhere between the serpent and the sin.

Creation 101 tells us that God the Creator made the heavens and the earth, light and dark, and separated the waters from both the sky and the lands. He made vegetation to grow out of the land and he separated day from night. Then came the creatures for the seas and birds for the sky.

Imagine it.

Five days of work and at the end of each day, the words "It is good." Then day six brings lots of work creating cows, rhinos, raccoons, giraffes, lions, and tigers, and bears... oh my! And God saw that it was good. Next up, and still during the waning hours of day six, God created his image-bearer—man. Does it spin anyone else around in your seat that after that amazing day of work, God's words do not reach a mountaintop crescendo of GOOD? Instead, the Creator looks at the last thing he has made, the man, and speaks the words, "It is not good for the man to be alone" (Gen. 2:18).

My farmer grandfather had a wonderful saying and I still hear his voice. When he wanted to sit with a thought for an extended amount of time, he would say, "Let's wallow in it." And usually after sitting still beside him as he wallowed over the matter, he would have something wonderfully wise to say. He would have allowed himself the time to "figure it out" or at least to see it from a different, perhaps more meaningful, point of view.

There was a peace about sitting beside my grandfather when he "wallowed" over something. There wasn't a striving or squirming; there was instead a desire to see it anew. No matter how old we get, our minds will remain youthful if we wisely try to see things in new ways. And while he only had a third-grade education, he became a very successful farmer, likely the result of lots of good wallowing. So rather than rush through that creation scene, let's wallow in it a bit...

The Creator knew the plans and purposes he had in forming the woman. He saw the need in the heart of the man; he was alone in this perfect garden. God knew this first woman could perfectly fill the aloneness. She was created to be that just-right fit for the man.

God wanted it to be clear why he was making this gift called woman. No matter how the world has defined her role, God, the One who made her, wanted it to be clear WHY he was creating her. God spoke of her identity when he named her.

From His Side

Since God is God, and he is omniscient, he knew humankind would be prone to warp and twist his reason for creating this gift. So he was meticulous as he created and named her. He did not make her in the same way he made Adam. Genesis 2:7 tells us that Adam was formed from the dust of the ground and God breathed into his nostrils and he became a living being.

The Hebrew word for man, adam, sounds like and may be related to the Hebrew word for ground, adamah. But Genesis 2:21–22 says, "God caused the man to fall into a deep sleep and while he was sleeping, God took one of the man's ribs and closed up the place with flesh. Then the Lord God made a woman from the rib he had taken out of the man, and he brought her to the man."

Adam came from the dust of the ground. Eve came from Adam's side. Do you think it possible that Adam saw the poetry of the gift? She was from him, bone and flesh; she was a part of him. She was not of the ground; she was of him, created for him from his side. Thousands of years later, Jesus' side would be pierced on the cross. In the garden, Adam's side was opened as well.

But Adam did not experience any pain in that first surgery. God put him to sleep in order to take Eve's beginnings from his side. Isn't it worth pondering that the Savior (the new Adam) experienced excruciating pain when his side was opened as he willingly gave his life to pay for the sins of the first Adam, as well as the sins of all humankind (Romans 5:12–17).

The One Who Made Her Called Her...

Maybe you've heard it before, but it's worth revisiting. The bone and flesh (v. 23) were not taken from Adam's head, implying she was above him, and they were not taken from his foot, implying she was beneath him. God chose to take the bone from Adam's side, signifying she was made to be beside him.

God did not allow Adam to watch her creation take place. It was a private matter between God and this gift to Adam. She was his daughter. Father's have special places in their hearts for their daughters. The Father feels deeply for his daughters as well.

Before all this took place, before she was formed and given as a gift to Adam, God had already called her by name. God did not give her the name Eve. Adam named the woman Eve (Gen. 3:20). It was before she was even created and in response to his own words, "It is not good for the man to be alone" that God gave a precise name to what he would create to alleviate Adam's aloneness.

He used two important words to describe her purpose beside Adam. The words would speak of her identity, not her name. Our Bibles today do not use those original Hebrew words spoken by God. Today's translations use words like "helper," "helpmate suitable," and "companion suitable." But when God first said it was not good for man to be alone, he used two Hebrew words to describe what was needed for Adam. God said he would make an *"ezer kenegdo."* An *ezer*, a helper. A *kenegdo*, one who is strong, even powerful, who is opposite of the man, who has a warrior-like way willing to stand beside the man and against evil.

Made for More

God's *ezer kenegdo* is one who will help the man stand against evil. Pause a moment here and think of the wives you know. Do they stand beside their husbands for the purpose of helping him stand against evil... evil working to wound their family... evil trying to damage their relationship? Can you see the strength of those women and the way their courage is being used to benefit their homes?

And think of other homes where you see the wife standing in opposition to her husband. Is it possible she is doing so because he is (knowingly or unknowingly) allowing some wrong to happen in their home? In their marriage? And, if so, in those moments of opposition, is she actually standing against her husband or is she standing against the thing that left undefeated will destroy the home she longs to protect and nurture? Warrior women who are trying to fight for what is good surround us. They are trying to protect the home. But have we seen it rightly?

Some women who have lost their way use the *kenegdo* strength inside them for their own selfish gain. Do you know any women like that? Women who want what they want and they'll do whatever they need to do to get it? These women are opening the door wide for evil to attack their homes. They don't understand (or sometimes they don't care) who they are supposed to be in their homes. They are ignoring why God made them.

Remember the woman at the beginning of this chapter? Walking down the street in the quaint seaport town, she was thinking of herself, not her home or her husband, not even about what was right or wrong. She was thinking of what she wanted—her way. She literally wanted her husband to "just give her what she wanted" so they could then be okay.

It's a sad trade she was willing to make. And even sadder still is the fact that she was in no way living up to the real purpose for which she was created. She was using her strength and her warrior-like ways to manipulate her husband into letting her have her way.

She would settle for an okay life getting what she wanted, rather than an amazing life beside her husband. To live this *ezer kenegdo* way, she wouldn't be getting what "she wanted" all the time. Rather, she would need to think about what was best for the whole of her home. She would need to ask herself, Is this thing I want good and right or is it not good and not right for the whole of our home?

She obviously didn't want to ask herself the challenging questions that would lead her toward making a wise decision. Instead, she wanted her husband to let her have her way and if he didn't, she would cause him trouble. That's a far cry from her call to be an *ezer kenegdo*.

The Pause, The Question

But what if, instead, she had "wallowed" in her desire for a few minutes. What if she had asked herself the right questions and allowed self-control and wisdom to guide her answers? Letting go of what she wanted for herself and looking more broadly at the big picture would have allowed wisdom to defeat selfishness, and she might not have been brawling on the sidewalk with her husband looking like a three-year-old throwing a tantrum. She could have blessed her husband with an honest conversation expressing her wants. There's nothing wrong with wanting something. It's what we do with those "wants" that determines our character. She could have allowed her husband to see her pause, question, and perhaps wallow in it a bit. She could have let him witness the process of her thinking through the rightness of her desired purchase or the realization that it was not necessary after all.

In expressing a want and then pausing, questioning, and processing long enough to choose the best outcome, respect could have grown between them. Sadly, though, the woman on the street that night was self-centered with no thought of being a "helper suitable." If she knew the real reason she was beside her husband, she might have been able to see the thunderclouds on the horizon as the MORE, the goodness of God's plans, slowly came into sight—more peace, more kindness, more self-control, more happiness—for both her husband and her. If the balance is not managed, then the scales will always tip to mean more for one and less for the other. This is not what God intended.

It sometimes feels as though we live life in our homes as if there's only a certain amount of love and goodness to give and receive.

We act like goodness in marriage is little more than chocolate cake on a plate. And we better get as big a slice as we can before it runs out. Marriage is not meant to be lived looking out for number one and every man for himself. It's meant to be a place where the artesian well of God's goodness flows between two people in infinite supply. The catch, or the valve, on the artesian well, though, is directly connected to being "open" to let good flow through us for the benefit of another. When two people are willing to let good flow through them for the benefit of the other, their home thrives! Does that sound a little "over the top" to you? Like maybe I'm crazy to write such a thing in a world where divorce rates continue to climb? If so, then perhaps we think that way only because we've seen so few real-life couples loving each other this way. It's what God intended. The chocolate cake doesn't have to run out or get old and grow fuzzy-looking mold on it. An *ezer kenegdo* living out her purpose and a man beside her living out his can be where goodness multiplies and hope begins to grow for those who see it.

But if either the *ezer* or the man beside her begins to focus on getting all they can, "Me first," "What's in this for me," "You owe me," "I deserve..." "If you'll just let me have my way" kinds of thinking, then the scales will tilt wildly, balance will be lost, and one of them will fade away while the other indulges. And their home will feel empty (no matter its size or contents). At least shooting stars look beautiful in their quick demise. Not so for the marriage that dies from the painful imbalance preceding its slow burn and burial.

Paul speaks clearly to this imbalance in Ephesians 5:21: "Submit to one another out of reverence for Christ." She submits to him and he submits to her out of reverence for Christ.

Now, don't worry. We're not denying the clear guidance of God's Word for wives to submit to their husbands. (We spend time addressing this in Chapter 8.) But in establishing a foundation for the book, we want to remember that in order to show reverence to Christ, there should be mutual submission between a man and the gift God gives him in a wife. Those are not our words. They come from the Creator through the pen of the apostle Paul in Ephesians.

Aloneness Can Happen, Even Beside Someone.

God made Eve for Adam because it was not good for Adam to be alone. Just as Eve is the mother of all women, Adam is the father of all men. If Eve were created to solve the aloneness in Adam's life, where does that leave the downtrodden man walking the old-seaport street behind his wife that evening?

He was most certainly a man, alone.

Just as medical students spend long hours and invest countless days studying, interning, and preparing for the day they will finally perform the surgery that saves a life, so it is for the woman beside a man working to stand against anything that would bring destruction to their relationship. Medical students don't get to do whatever they want. They must do the right thing for the patient. And aren't we thankful when doctors do the right things for us?

Likewise for a wife. She can't do whatever she wants. She must do what she knows is the right thing for her home, for her husband, even for herself—the inner woman, the *ezer kenegdo* she was created to be. And everyone fortunate to live in her home, including her, will be blessed.

"If you want something in your life you've never had, you'll have to do something you've never done." ~Anonymous

"Who Is This Coming Up from the Wilderness Leaning on Her Beloved?" (Song of Solomon 8:5)

I've always loved this verse in Song of Solomon. It encourages and inspires me in many ways. It's life giving to know that I can emerge from the "wilderness of life" and step into a new place (out of the darkness). To successfully emerge, I must be found leaning on my beloved. Some might think the word "beloved" is referring to a man, a husband. Not me. While I love Steve dearly, and I do lean on him in some ways, this wilderness emergence will find me leaning on my first love, my Savior, the One who died for me. It is only HE who can save me in the wilderness, walking me out of darkness and allowing me to lean on him as I find the clean, clear air of a new place. No more wilderness confusion or fear. Instead, with him I find a new way, a new me, who is better able to be what he had intended all along.

The doctor goes to medical school to learn, the lawyer to law school. The woman must go to God. She must learn from the One who calls her an *ezer kenegdo*. What does he really mean? What does that look like in the eyes of the One who made her?

Before we can step into becoming what God intended us to be, let's be honest about just how badly it has gone wrong. Buckle yourself in. The next section of the road is not a pleasant ride, but we've got to get through the deep mud before we can head to higher ground.

Chapter 2

Too Far from the Garden

The dandelion has been used by humans for food and for herbal purposes for much of recorded history. Every part of the flower, from root to petal, is edible. And yet, all too often, it is dug up and thrown away as an unwanted weed.

On the Side of the Mountain

The women surrounding me in the small, dirt-floor church were strong and, dare I say, intimidating. Their hands were calloused, their faces stern. They carried babies on their backs and the weight of life on their shoulders. They had asked me to come to their side of the mountain to help them with something they knew they needed but could not find their way to—*forgiveness.*

I sat in the dark room with my Bible in my hand and teaching notes on the table. I was ready with illustrations that were culturally appropriate, all prayed up and eager to teach. But my knees went weak. It was their eyes... their strong, sad eyes that shook my heart loose and lodged it in my throat. Without a word, their eyes spoke—no, they screamed into the silence of the room. They were hungry for something that would not fill their stomachs; their souls were longing to be filled.

These lessons on forgiveness would not be for their heads alone. Their hearts ached and their insides cried out. They had known unspeakable pain and they had survived. No one had told me about the depth of the pain. The heaviness in the room broke my heart, and I didn't yet know the fullness of their wounds. But later that evening, their stories filled the night air around me.

They were exhausted from abuse, drained from long years of hard work, bearing children, burying loved ones, mending wounds, hiding from rebels. These women had buried family members under the fields they now grew maize on, and they'd remained silent through it all. When killing comes like a hurricane, there is no time for propriety. Some of their children had lost the ability to speak when their eyes saw the evil that had entered their huts.

And I was to teach them about forgiving others.

On My Knees

Moving to Kenya months prior had rocked my world and awakened me. We had traveled to Africa several times serving in various places, but when we moved there to live and serve full time, we realized how very little we knew about the continent and its people. Suffering was common. Need was normal. Wants were rarely considered. Survival was every day's headline.

That day in the little church packed with dozens of wounded warrior women, I realized how little I knew about women, about life. My childhood had been so different than theirs; different latitudinal and longitudinal lines had held blue skies over extremely different worlds. While I'd been learning to bake cakes and iron clothes, they had been learning to endure hunger and stay strong. We both had been learning to be submissive to men.

For me this meant cooking dinner, caring for the home, praying for my husband, and supporting him as the God-ordained leader in our home. For them it had meant something completely different. Their submission required them to give of themselves day and night to men who were not expected to remain faithful, provide for their families, or control their angry hands. Submission for these ladies meant, "He is stronger but somehow you must survive whatever he chooses to do to you and his children, and you must survive in silence."

These ladies had so much to forgive. Surely the plants in the fields surrounding us had no need of rain. Tears had watered them. These were strong women who helped their children survive and held onto one another when drunken husbands did their worst, all this in the name of submission.

The Submissive Ezer—It Was the Plan...

In her book Half the Church, Carolyn Custis James opens eyes with her beautiful depiction of the Father's heart for his first daughter, Eve. She writes,

> *"Events surrounding the creation of the first woman lead me to believe God harbors strong sentiments for his daughters. He greets his first daughter's entry into his story with not a little fanfare and, in naming her, chooses a name that binds her and all his daughters to himself in a special way. God calls the first woman ezer, a name that is used most frequently in the Old Testament for God himself. In a profound sense, God named his firstborn daughter after himself. God is Israel's ezer. For God's female image bearers, ezer defines a way in which women are uniquely called to reflect God. 'Like Father, like daughter,' as the saying goes. Our Father is an ezer, and we are ezers too."*

Ezer is commonly interpreted to mean helper in modern translations of the Bible. But as I looked into the lives of these ladies living on a mountainside in Africa, it stung my soul that these beautiful *ezer*s had been abused by men who thought they had the right to beat submission into their "helpers," sadly using the Bible wrongly as one of their most potent hammers. They declared they would beat the woman who spoke out against her husband, just as Adam (in their opinion) should have beaten Eve into silence. It's for those women still working and forgiving on the mountain that this must be shared.

God gave his reason for creating his first daughter. A quick review of the previous chapter reminds us again.

It was not good for man to be alone; he needed a helper, an *ezer*. And this helper needed to be a fit for, suited for, comparable to him. No animal that had been created could fill the role. Nothing in the garden was able to meet Adam's need. God was with Adam, so some might dispute that he was alone. But God himself declared there was still an aloneness that was not good for Adam. God knew he had created Adam with a need for relationship. Relationship with God is a vertical connection that can touch the soul of man. But there remains the heart, the feelings, and the emotions of man that are designed by God for a relationship with another soul-carrying image bearer (not an animal, but a person).

God's plan was exquisite in every way. This human relationship with the one who would solve the problem of aloneness would also be equipped to fit perfectly in other ways as the "two became one." And this physical union would allow for more soul-carrying image bearers to be born. The Creator would vertically pour his goodness into the horizontal relationships between husbands and wives and even the children they would produce together.

Eve was to solve Adam's aloneness and she did—immediately. Adam claimed her as his own, bone of his bone and flesh of his flesh. And they were naked and unashamed together in the garden (Gen. 2:23–25). This was the culmination of God's work of creation in the Garden found at the end of Genesis 2. The Creator's grand finale was beautiful. All of earth and its creatures were in place—one for all and all for the ONE. It was right.

But the first verses of Genesis 3 describe this perfect garden under a stealthy attack... quiet, sly, and potent. Have we overlooked the chain of events? Did we miss the timing of the serpent's arrival? Did we think it mere coincidence that immediately after the gift of Eve, the *ezer kenegdo*, we read the disturbing words, "Now the serpent...'"?

Here we've come to another moment where wallowing is most appropriate. We need to see it thoroughly, clearly, and perhaps from another angle all together.

The Attack—Not on a Mountainside, Not in a Garden, but Much, Much Closer

Growing up in my home, never once did my father imply that my mother was wicked or evil. Instead, I saw how he treasured her for the gift she was. Other men might have looked down on their wives, but not my father. He seemed to appreciate my mother as an *ezer kenegdo* long before he knew of the Hebrew words. My mother's input was requested when making major (or sometimes even minor) decisions. In the end, it was my father who would bear the weight of the decisions made in our home, but my mother was right there beside him—working, praying, cleaning, and caring for our home. But as I grew older, I came to realize that not all men walked as uprightly as my dad. Abuse was common, neglect overlooked, and unfaithfulness in the eyes of some seemed almost normal... even expected.

Education opened my eyes wider as new friends in college shared their heartbreaking stories of infidelity and separation between their parents, sometimes even abuse and divorce. Late-night talks in our dorm rooms became safe places for deep hurts to erupt. And those who hurt the most knew they were willingly playing into the hands of young men who would use them. These were wounded daughters who had grown into beautiful young women hoping to cover their fear of being unwanted by giving the guys what they wanted. Those painful one-night stands could be more easily forgotten if they drank enough to numb their minds, so sometimes they did just that. But in the quiet of the dark hours, when they lay there alone, they felt like little girls again who wondered if Daddy was coming home, if their homes (if they) would survive. And the thought of becoming an *ezer kenegdo* was as distant as the far-off galaxies on a moonless night.

There was little difference between the women on the mountain in Africa and the girls on the campus in college. They both were being stripped of their ability to "see" who they were created to be. Stripped in different ways, but each of them was wounded and left exposed, unable to be who she was born to be.

One day after class, a friend walked into my dorm room. She wore sunglasses inside our room and spoke in whispering tones as if she were revealing a secret. My roommate asked her what was wrong. She slowly sunk to the edge of the bed and forced the words to come, "I love him so much; it's really my fault. I should never make him angry. I should be more careful to do what he tells me to do."

We were dumbfounded as our beautiful friend shared her sad story. Her military cadet boyfriend was beating her when she even spoke to another male student, and she was convinced it was her fault. We rallied around her and did our best to help her remember that she was a person with a right to talk with others. But in the end, she shriveled under his shadow, married him, and moved to Germany with him. Her reasoning was that her father had left her mother when she was a small girl, and she had vowed to her own frightened little self that she would do whatever she needed to do to keep her someday-husband from leaving her. She feared abandonment more than she feared abuse. I've often wondered how life turned out for her.

The stories are numerous and cover all countries and classes. It's not just on the rugged mountainside in Africa or in the more polished homes of America. It's e-v-e-r-y-w-h-e-r-e. Wives who fear the stigma of being deserted will endure the heartbreak of wrong treatment, all in hopes that their husbands won't leave them.

Moving to Africa opened doorways to painful stories of abuse and desertion as women worked to fill the stomachs of their children while fathers abandoned them and often took other wives. But to be clear, it was not the first time I had witnessed the intense damage the serpent had inflicted when he made his first appearance years ago in a perfect garden just hours after the first union of man and woman.

The Attack – Twisted Words

Living in Kenya, we found that many would claim to be Christians, attending church, even holding the Bible in their hands. But they used it as a weapon of justification for their behavior. They distorted the Scriptures to fit their own personal agendas, silencing their wives, indulging in whatever they wanted. The words often used were, "I am the lion of my home. I will have what I want when I want it. Even God says I am the head of this house." The wife prepared meals, cared for the children, tended the farm, washed, cooked, and gave herself to her husband even if she knew he had been with others already. One mother shared of the day she had been required to give her daughter over to the "lion's" bed. Otherwise, he would leave and she would be forced into prostitution to feed the children. For her it seemed that sacrificing one to his bed was better than watching them all starve.

How could it ever have gone so wrong?

We must remember, the "serpent" did not actually care about the fruit in the garden. No, his sights were on the destruction of the relationships—Adam and Eve's relationship with God and with each other. And make no mistake; the enemy's target is still set on the destruction of every relationship because he wants to defeat the gifts God desires to give in those relationships. What God had intended for good, the enemy of God wanted to destroy. What God intends for good today, the deceiver still wants to destroy.

The wording in more recent English translations of the Bible refers to the woman as a helper. And self-indulgent, domineering, lion-like men declare how the wife can best "help," and, if not carefully managed, dominance gives way to abuse. None of this is what God intended when he created Eve to solve the problem of Adam's aloneness. God clearly defined in the very word *ezer* that she would be a most valuable helper, but humankind has too often overruled his plans.

It's a serpent of a different sort than the one who appeared in the garden. It's a serpent of deceit and selfishness, self-centeredness and entitlement. Too often "the serpent" still comes on the scene when women and men are joined in marriage. That serpent has never forgotten his assignment against homes.

The Attack – Clever Words

When God created an *ezer* for man, he knew the serpent was about to show itself. Nothing is a mystery to God; nothing catches him by surprise. God knew that the ultimate gift in the garden would be the *ezer*. And this gift would in time begin to reveal much about God's love for humankind. The serpent knew this gift, this union, had the potential to solidify the goodness of God in the hearts of humankind. Therefore, the timing of the serpent's arrival was not by chance.

When Adam received his *ezer*, the deceiver knew he needed to do something to damage the relationships that were forming between God and humankind and between man and woman. So his first plan was to make God appear to be a liar: "You will not surely die if you eat of this fruit, instead you will become like God..." And not recorded in Scripture, but perhaps thoughts in his scaly head—*While I'm at it, I better do something to break this joyous union of the man and the woman. Too much good could come if I don't mess this up, so I'll deceive the weaker of the two, the one who didn't actually hear with her own ears the instructions God gave to Adam. I'll trick her, and, hopefully, the man will stand silently while I draw her in and make her wonder if perhaps Adam misunderstood God's instructions. If the man will stay silent, then I can deceive her more easily, and if she will offer the fruit to him after she's tasted it and not died before his eyes, then I can deceive them both.*

It was a clever ploy to destroy all those first relationships because the enemy of our Lord knows if he can destroy relationships, he can destroy homes. If he can destroy homes, he can destroy lives. And if he can destroy lives, the goodness of God will not be seen and love will lose, all because, "Now, the serpent was more crafty..." (Gen. 3:1 NIV).

Adam had not encountered the deceiver in the form of the serpent or in any other form until the woman was created. The woman herself was not evil; she was God's good gift for Adam, bone of his bones and flesh of his flesh (Gen. 2:23 NIV). But God knew the serpent would be coming and he knew Adam would need a helper. God knew they would need each other because he knew what was to come. God knew man would need to stand beside his *ezer* and she would need to stand beside him in order to stand strong against the deceiver, speaking truth to each other, supporting each other, encouraging each other, and reminding each other of God's instructions.

Imagine what might have happened during that first garden encounter with the serpent if Adam had stepped forward and said, "Eve, no, we will not listen to this serpent. We will obey God."

Adam was with Eve when she took the fruit and ate it: "She took some and ate it. She also gave some to her husband, who was with her, and he ate it" (Gen. 3:6, emphasis added). What a great story it would have been if Adam had stood beside Eve and reminded her of the words God had spoken to him, if they had chosen to obey God and stand firm together.

Adam was not helpless. He was simply silent. Perhaps Adam doubted God's words as well, and he thought to himself, *Let's just see if she dies or not; then I'll know better whom to believe.*

We don't know if Eve would have tossed the fruit down and walked away from the serpent if only Adam had spoken up. She might have responded with a heartfelt appreciation of Adam and a strong obedience to God. We will never know.

Adam did not have to take and eat the fruit Eve offered to him. He could have said, "No, Eve, you have disobeyed the instructions God gave. I am sorry you have made that choice, but I will not join you in this wrong. Perhaps God will forgive you or perhaps you will die. But I will not go along with this disobedience."

Imagine how the rest of Genesis might look, the rest of the Bible. God might have disciplined Eve alone. He might have destroyed her and created another *ezer kenegdo* that would be more obedient. He might have forgiven her disobedience and spoken more clearly to her of his instructions.

Adam was not helpless. Eve was deceived. Adam willingly complied. Both sinned; both were ashamed; both hid from God.

The Attack Continues

And thus goes the story of humankind from then until now. We hide from God, blame others, feel ashamed, but still all too often listen to the deceiver and doubt God. He knew this would be the plight of humankind. And he knew it would not be good for man to be alone in it. So he gave him a helper, an *ezer*, who would need the help of the man she was created for. Eve was Adam's *ezer*. God planned it so they would both need HIM, and they would best be able to face the coming serpent if they stood together.

There are women on the side of a mountain in Africa, in the paved cul-de-sac suburbs of America, and along every pathway found in every part of the world working to forgive the wrongs done against them and their homes. They know intensely the damage done when that first serpent spoke. They've suffered at the hands of modern-day Adams, who leave them to fend for themselves and then blame them when things go wrong. The weight is too much for them. But, amazingly, they still long to be *ezer*s. They are trying. Hope is struggling inside their warrior-like hearts.

> "Surely this ought to transform how Christian men view and value women and girls. Surely it ought to transform what men consider when choosing a wife and how a husband regards his wife—not as dependent, but as a strong and indispensible ally who shares with him the battles and the burdens of life." —Carolyn Custis James *(Half the Church)*

Too Far from the Garden

Chapter 3

The Ezer and the Preacher

The dandelion's taproot brings up nutrients for the shallower-rooting plants and adds minerals and nitrogen to the soil. An ezer kenegdo does the same for those around her.

It Is a Possibility

I watched her old hands work the dough, form the round balls, and pat them down gently onto the well-greased pan; it was like a slow dance. She'd let me sit on the counter beside her so I could watch every detail. I loved her. Still do. And she knew it. Her tiny kitchen window was usually open; little yellow curtains grabbed bits of breeze and joined in the dancing that always happened in her kitchen. She knew how to create a medley of music in the silence of her peaceful world, and I was her eager little audience. Whatever my grandmother did, it was slow and steady and safe. She moved with grace. Never fast. I never once saw her do anything fast. But she always had everything done and in such a way that made the efforts of others seem somehow sloppy (mine included). She wasn't trying to do anything better than others. She just lived so well. It was as if she was unknowingly always positioned in the middle of a grand stage. Whatever she did, it was worth watching closely. She taught best without words. She lived what textbooks could not hold.

There was a rhythm in the way time passed around her. Flowers grew in tidy beds, laundry fluttered on the line, the sun shined just right in her backyard, and if goodness ever chose where to take its midday nap, I'm certain it was under the oaks beside her tiny country home. All this happened daily. Those who came near her were blessed. I wanted to be just like her when I grew up.

My grandfather was a fortunate man. He had married her when she was only 15 years old (both consenting, both in love). And she had likewise chosen very well when she scooted up beside him for the rest of her life. Having a part of them flowing through my veins is a gift most undeserved.

Not everyone does life so well. We all have stories we could tell of those who did not live in life-giving ways. And for some, the odds of life seemed to weigh too heavily against them and they were never able to get their noses above the ever-rising waterline. We hear those stories often. The previous chapter visited many tear-filled places. But sometimes it might be that we have golden treasures in our lives that we don't pause long enough to notice. Living well equals noticing the treasure people around us. Who are the golden souls in your world? Do they know you see them that way?

They were beautiful together. They were also lovely apart. But when you put them together, the air rested well around them. She'd slide the biscuit pan into the oven; he'd be choosing which plates we'd eat our breakfast from. She'd count out the napkins; he'd fold them just right. She'd spoon fresh fruit into their little frosted dessert dishes; he'd carry the homemade jams to the table. Some might say their routines were mechanical and boring, not exciting enough. They would be woefully wrong. For their living was like a flawless musical with an ever-attentive private audience. And to this day, I'm still applauding.

She was the key to his lock. He was the nut to her bolt. And he would be the first to laugh at that last sentence. She was the picture; he was the nail it hung on. He was the floor; she was the rug that decorated it. She was the laundry, he was the clothespin; he was the rod, she was the line. They planned it that way. It didn't just happen. They each shifted as they needed to for the sake of the other. And it was beautiful. They lived the words. "Submit to one another out of reverence for Christ" (Ephesians 5:21 NIV).

He was a preacher. She sang in the choir. He was often gone caring for those in need. She was busy cooking something for him to carry with him. He dug into God's Word through the week; she dug into prayers for the sermon he'd share on Sunday.

It was beautiful.

Many years later, long after my dear grandparents had passed on, I would continue learning from them. No one is perfect, this we all know. But the way they lived continues to teach decades after they finished their living, and that speaks volumes in a world that flounders. My grandmother was a lovely *ezer kenegdo* for my grandfather. She filled the space of aloneness brought to his life; she was a helper. But she was so much more. She was meant to be more than just a helper and a person to fill the space beside him. She was more. If only my grandfather could share it in his own words with us now.

Focusing on the Ezer Part

Genesis 2:18 says, "It is not good for the man to be alone, I will make...

- A helper suitable (NIV) (NASB)
- A help meet (KJV) (ASV)
- A helper just right for him (NLT)
- A helper, a companion (MSG)
- A helper comparable to him (NKJV)

- A helper (one who balances him, a counterpart) suitable and complementary for him (AMP)

- The companion he needs, one just right for him (ERV)

There are varying ways the Hebrew word *ezer* can be interpreted into our less thorough English of today. It's an interesting word study that has been pursued often by those much more scholarly than me. I am not a theologian or a biblical scholar, but I am a seeker, a learner. How thankful I am for those who have delved into the mysteries of Hebrew and Greek word studies. There are some altering views on specific meanings (and there are some who have attempted to coerce the interpretation to meet their own desires, which you will NOT find shared in this book). But as I have studied extensively with a wholehearted desire to grasp the TRUTH of the words, here is a portion of what I've discovered.

The word *ezer* (noun) is found 21 times in the Old Testament. In the Scripture references below, I have replaced the word "help/helper" with *ezer* so you can grasp the intended meaning in the verses.

> Genesis 2:18, 20: ¹⁸ *"The LORD God said, "It is not good for the man to be alone. I will make an ezer suitable for him." ²⁰ "So the man gave names to all the livestock, the birds in the sky and all the wild animals. But for Adam no suitable ezer was found."*

> Daniel 11:34: *"When they fall, they will receive an ezer"* (referring to military aid to come).

> Isaiah 30:5: *"Who bring neither ezer nor advantage, but only shame and disgrace."* (Referring to military aid being needed)

> Ezekiel 12:14: *"I will scatter to the winds all those around him—his staff and all his troops—and I will pursue them with drawn sword."* (The help/*ezer* is coming through

military support.)

Exodus 18:4: *"Eliezer [which means my God is helper], for he said, 'My father's God was my ezer; he saved me from the sword of Pharaoh.'"* (Referring to God as a helper who saves)

Deuteronomy 33:7: *"Hear, O Lord, the cry of Judah; bring him to his people. With his own hands he defends his cause. Oh, be his ezer against his foes!"* (Referring to God as a helper against enemies)

Deuteronomy 33:26: *"There is no one like the God of Jeshurun, who rides on the heavens to ezer you and on the clouds in his majesty."* (Referring to God riding on the heavens to come and help)

Deuteronomy 33:29: *"Blessed are you, Israel! Who is like you, a people saved by the Lord? He is your shield and ezer and your glorious sword."* (Referring to God as a protector)

Psalm 20:2: *"May he send you an ezer from the sanctuary and grant you support from Zion."* (Referring to God as a helper)

Psalm 33:20 - *"We wait in hope for the Lord; he is our ezer and our shield."* (Referring to God as our help)

Psalm 70:5: *"But as for me, I am poor and needy; come quickly to me, O God. You are my ezer and my deliverer; Lord, do not delay."* (Referring to God as our helper)

Psalm 89:19: *"Once you spoke in a vision, to your faithful people you said: 'I have bestowed ezer (strength) on a warrior; I have exalted a young man from among the people.'"*

(Referring to help that comes through the strength God sends)

Psalm 115:9: *"O house of Israel, trust in the Lord – He is your ezer and shield."* (Referring to God as the helper of Israel)

Psalm 115:10: *"O house of Aaron, trust in the Lord – He is your ezer and shield."* (Referring to God as the helper of Aaron)

Psalm 115:11: *"You who fear him, trust in the Lord – He is your ezer and shield."* (Referring to God as the helper for those who fear and trust him)

Psalm 121:1: *"I lift up my eyes to the hills – where does my ezer come from?"* (Referring to God as the helper)

Psalm 121:2: "My *ezer* comes from the Lord, the Maker of heaven and earth." (Referring to God as the helper)

Psalm 124:8: "Our *ezer* is in the name of the Lord, the Maker of heaven and earth." (Referring to God as our help)

Psalm 146:5: *"Blessed is he whose ezer is the God of Jacob, whose hope is in the Lord his God."* (Referring to God as the helper)

Hosea 13:9: *"You are destroyed, O Israel, because you are against me, against your ezer."* (Referring to God as the helper)

Twice *ezer* refers to Eve.

Three times *ezer* refers to military support (or the need of it).

The remaining sixteen times we see the word *"ezer"* used in the Bible, it is referring to God as our help, helper, or protector.

Bringing the Ezer Out of the Garden

Why do little girls not grow up learning the importance of their namesake? God gave the first woman (and every woman) her purpose and identity when he said that man needed an *ezer kenegdo* beside him. God proved her place was beside him; she was formed from his side. But in the very name she was given, so much was being communicated to a world where serpents slither and deceit destroys.

The Creator gave the woman the very name he would allow to be used to refer to himself —Ezer. The same name is used when referring to military strategy and support. Modern interpretations will say *ezer* simply means helper. There is no disputing that *ezer* does mean helper. But why did we allow it to end there when it means so much more?

Ezer refers also to support and aid as found in military strategies and victories. When attacks are being planned and battles are underway, an *"ezer"* is needed—one who will help, one who will come even when the battle is at its worst and the enemy seems to be winning. An *ezer* in battle is brave, strong, courageous, and able to make a difference. What woman grows up knowing she carries within her the ability to be an *ezer kenegdo*?

Sixteen times the Creator—the King—the One who is above all things (1 Chronicles 29:11, NLT) is referred to as an *ezer*. God lines the woman-*ezer* up with himself as he tries to clarify through the very use of the word what kind of "helper" the woman will be to the man. She will be God's image-bearing daughter and others will see him in her strength and courage and devotion.

In researching for this writing, sadly we found that some women work to twist the use of the word and begin viewing themselves as a type of god, declaring the first woman was a god, and since God also used the word *ezer* to refer to himself, he was saying she would have the power of a god. This is dangerous territory, and we soundly renounce that way of thinking. God is God and there is NO OTHER. So to be clear, we do NOT agree with this teaching. Women who have suffered at the hands of men and are working to find ways to dominate their oppressors most often adopt this belief. This is not the correct use of the word "*ezer*."

The fact that God called the first woman an *ezer kenegdo* does not elevate her above the man into a god-like position. Instead, God's choosing to call her an *ezer kenegdo* is his beautiful way of letting all know that she carries his name inside her and as he is our helper for good, she too will be a helper for good. She will be like God in this way, and the man beside her will be blessed because of it.

Yet another excerpt from Half the Church by Carolyn Custis James puts it this way:

> *"Putting the facts together, isn't it obvious that the ezer is a warrior? And don't we already know this in our bones? God created His daughters to be ezer-warriors with our brothers. He deploys the ezer to break the man's loneliness by soldiering with him wholeheartedly and at full strength for God's gracious kingdom.*
>
> *The man needs everything she brings to their*

global mission.

Other factors confirmed my conclusions. Of course, the strength God brings as ezer to His people should be sufficient to convince us that as ezers we must be strong, resourceful, alert to the cries of the needy and oppressed, and proactive too."

If In Doubt, Seek It Out

Ladies, read through the Scriptures yourselves. The Creator of the universe calls his daughters by a name he calls himself, and HE is the one who gave the name to us. Gentlemen, read them as well, and perhaps look at your wives, daughters, sisters, and mothers with eyes more clearly aligned with how they are seen by the God who made them.

It's one of the secrets my grandfather took to his rest. He knew the beautiful gift of the *ezer* who lived beside him. She was his helper, but she was more than that. There was a powerful strength in her gentle ways, and yet I always sensed she could be fierce if needed. She was a rock that would not be moved from the place she knew she was to be. Her place was beside him, but not to be his doormat, not to be his maid, not to be his controller, and not to be his boss. Her place was beside him to stand as an image bearer, a light carrier, a companion who would weather the storms of life praying for him (knowing the serpent still lurks about), protecting him (from those who would try and wound their home), supporting him (when life's disappointing winds blew too hard), and enjoying him (celebrating together what they had accomplished side by side).

She was his greatest fan and his strongest ally. She was also his closest confidant and his strictest accountability partner. Too many women talk too much outside the home and don't pay close enough attention to what's happening inside their homes. A confidant only shares what can be used for good purposes and to honor God. An *ezer* will be this for her husband and her home. She will be a safe place of confidentiality. My grandmother knew how to protect her home in this way, and my grandfather treasured her safe counsel and wisdom.

Neither of them could be certain the other was always doing the right thing; decisions can be tricky sometimes. But standing beside each other (not broadcasting to others) and working together to do the next right thing (holding each other accountable) in every area of their lives meant they each could help the other fly straighter because they were balancing each other.

Unbalanced Loads Crash

In the Garden of Eden, when the serpent appeared, Eve made a decision on her own with no mention of her seeking God for guidance or her husband for his input. She then invited Adam to join her in the choice she had made. They flew crooked. No balance. They crashed.

How different it would have looked if they had helped each other stand in better ways. Not to get what each wanted. Not to have his or her own way. Not even to try and outsmart each other or the One who made them. How differently the story of life would be if that first husband and wife had helped each other stand in the way that was right.

It Is Possible

Perhaps reading about my *ezer* grandmother has left you wondering, How? Even I often wondered to myself, How did she do it so well? She made it look easy. But how? Then the good response to her beautiful example comes flowing through. To remember her for the inspiration she was and not compare myself to her is the right response.

My dear grandmother was not a lady who compared herself to others. She was content with being who she was, and she was happy to allow others to be who they were. Even this remembrance of her is inspiring. She would not want you or me to compare ourselves to her—never. Instead, she would most assuredly want us to take from her what would benefit us and leave the rest in the past. Too often we look at others and measure ourselves. This is toxic thinking. Instead, we need to be so focused on who God made us to be that we expend all our energies on achieving that good place in ourselves and in our homes.

Comparing ourselves to others, even to the memories I've shared here of my grandmother, will always throw our life loads off balance! Don't do it. Don't look at another and measure yourself according to her accomplishments, appearance, title, or lifestyle. However, if you can look at a good example another has given by the way she has lived well and left the world better, then you are wise to let her inspire you to reach for the more you, too, are capable of.

For most of my adult life, I've read everything I could find about Ruth Bell Graham, Mother Teresa, and Corrie ten Boom. These three women, in my mind, stand head and shoulders above the rest of the pack. They each were uniquely committed, wholeheartedly focused, and beautifully successful in their accomplishments. One married, two did not, and all three were extraordinary *ezer kenegdo*s! It is one of the reasons I feel so strongly that every woman is created to be an *ezer kenegdo*. Whether she lives out her identity from God in her own home with a husband and children, in a ministry caring for souls in need, or through writing and teaching to a worldwide audience, she is still an *ezer kenegdo* working to alleviate the sense of aloneness. I have never compared myself to any of these three "greats," but I have allowed them to inspire me to the point of becoming a travel guide, a goal setter, a whisperer in my ear that says, "It is possible to rise above the madness of this world and live well."

My grandmother, Emma Glover, was my up-close inspiration as well. She did not try to be someone else. Instead she focused very carefully on being who God made her to be, and it is my hope that she will inspire you as well. So, do not let the serpent slither into your thoughts whispering lies of comparison or thoughts like, It might have worked for her, but it can't for me. Don't be an Eve-in-the-garden today listening to the deceiver. Instead, please hear the truth and good news of this chapter. God created e-v-e-r-y woman with a clear, concise, and wonderful purpose. She is to be his namesake and help a man alone or a lonely world in ways that will show his goodness to a lost and troubled world.

The main difference between them—Ruth, Teresa, Corrie, and Emma—and others is that they chose to focus on the One who made them and what he said about them. The world could not pull them down; their sights were on the higher way. Not one of them drove a fine car, lived in a mansion, obtained countless degrees, or focused on her appearance. They were too busy making a difference in the world, beginning with those beside them.

Chapter 4

Digging in the Garden

*It's Latin name, Taraxacum, originates in medieval Persian
writings and was used for pharmaceutical purposes. The
French name was dent-de-lion, meaning lion's tooth. This
name was derived from the jagged edges of its green foliage.
Most commonly, it is now simply called "dandelion" in
English. Here we find the perfect example: the name may
have changed, but the value and purpose of the flower
remains the same.*

The Damage or the Blessing; It Can Go Either Way

His clothes spoke of success; his demeanor conveyed defeat. This man was worn to a frazzle underneath his crisply pressed collar. Few understood why. The home he shared with his wife was palatial, well groomed, and the envy of many. He had worked hard for many years to provide well. He loved his wife; she was what he treasured most. Not a day had ever passed that their home was out of order. She prided herself on her ability to have a good meal on the table, children clean and well behaved, laundry done, and calendared events in order for the next six months. If it was dirty, she washed it. If it was crooked, she straightened it. If it was smelly, she perfumed it. If it was unsightly, she hid it. She was a helper extraordinaire. She was the epitome of what some might think to be the perfect "helper suitable" in a home.

But there was something very wrong. Everything "looked" perfect on the outside, but there was a lurking darkness, a lingering stench. It had to do with matters of the heart that grew inside this helper-wife. She was fixated on how things looked on the outside, but was unable to address how things actually were on the inside, where her scrub brushes couldn't reach. She was a controller, and she had not nurtured and cared for those living inside her home. How they looked and behaved mattered more than what they felt or believed.

Having grown up in church, she had purposed in her heart to be the most submissive wife and the best partner for the husband she chose. She wanted to do it all just right, but even she knew something was missing. They should have glowed with happiness. They had everything a person could possibly want. But there was a heaviness that weighed them down. Now, before any needling thoughts fester that I'm being critical of this fictional, but all-too-real person, let me settle it here. I've known many ladies like her. But most of all, I've been her, ashamed of it I am. (Chapter 5 tells our not-so-pretty story.)

Just a few miles away was another beautiful home with the happiest of people living within its walls. This house was beautiful, as well, but there was a kind goodness about it that made you want to step into the light that beamed through its windows in the late evening. The lady of this house was not perfect in appearance, but her welcoming warmth filled the house. Her husband was a happy man, strong, confident, and sure of himself. He was one of the gentlest men in their community. Her children laughed beside her; her husband was eager to come home; she carried nothing inside her that wounded others; she was a safe haven and a lighthouse for any who paused at her door. But she could be tough as nails. The order and uprightness of her home was the result of the order and uprightness of her soul. She held firmly with what was good and would go to battle against what was not if she sensed it trying to cross the threshold of her home. There was a strength and goodness to her that made those near her feel as if they were wearing life vests in a boat. No matter the condition of the waters surrounding them, she was a place of peace and security. (This is not a fictional home. It's the real home of a lifelong *ezer*-friend.)

I've known several of these homes, but not many. May their numbers increase.

The first home had an *ezer*, a helper, a manager, but there was nothing more. She was strong and yes, she had a warrior-like way, but warriors have the capacity to wound their own comrades if not careful. Friendly fire can destroy a home faster than lightning. It looked right, but those inside that home knew something was wrong.

The second home had an *ezer kenegdo* watching over it. Everyone within its walls knew the outside matched the inside, and love covered it all. This is the "more" my grandfather saw in my grandmother. She was an *ezer*, yes, but she was so much more.

It Takes Both—the Ezer and the Kenegdo

When God saw that it was not good for man to be alone, he created an *ezer kenedgo* to be the solution for this aloneness. The original language used in Genesis did not speak of a "helper-suitable." It used the words *ezer kenegdo*. In the steps of translating from Hebrew to English, so much has been missed.

As a young woman, I had watched closely the many different ways women lived beside their husbands and cared for their children and homes. Why did I watch so closely? Because even at a young age, my heart's longing was to become a wife and mother. My pursuits of education were framed around learning ways I could best bless my someday husband and children. This longing to be a blessing in my own home was what transformed every home into a classroom for me. I'd watch closely and ask many questions. To be clear, I never watched to be critical—never. I watched to learn. Then I'd watch to see how the family interacted with one another. Even in those days, perhaps God was preparing me for this work you now hold.

It wasn't until I was over 40 that I first heard the words "*ezer kenegdo*." I'd grown up in the church, but had only heard the words "helper suitable or helpmate" when referring to what the wife was to be for her husband according to Genesis 2. There is no critical tone to my words, only an honest revealing that even growing up in the church doesn't mean we will receive the fullness of what God's Word holds. We must seek in order to find. Reading Stasi and John Elderidge's book Captivating was a wonderful, eye-opening experience. How refreshing to read someone's unshielded revelations concerning the heart of a woman. I leaned forward when I came to page 31 in their book. The words "*ezer kenegdo*" entered stage left onto the scene—and I was both dumbfounded and frustrated. To convey it accurately, here's what I read:

> *"When God creates Eve, He calls her an ezer kenegdo. 'It is not good for the man to be alone, I shall make him [an ezer kenegdo]' (Gen. 2:18)."*
> *Hebrew scholar Robert Alter, who has spent years translating the book of Genesis, says that this phrase is "notoriously difficult to translate." The various attempts we have in English are "helper" or "companion" or the notorious "helpmeet." Why are these translations so incredibly wimpy, boring, flat... disappointing? What is a helpmeet, anyway? What little girl dances through the house singing, "One day I shall be a helpmeet?" Companion? A dog can be a companion. Helper? Sounds like Hamburger Helper. Alter is getting closer when he translates it 'sustainer beside him.'*

"The word 'ezer' is used only twenty other places in the entire Old Testament. And in every other instance, the person being described is God Himself, when you need Him to come through for you desperately.

"Blessed are you, O Israel! Who is like you, a people saved by the Lord? He is your shield and helper and your glorious sword" (Deuteronomy 33:26, 29).

"I lift up my eyes to the hills—where does my help come from? My help comes from the Lord, the Maker of heaven and earth" (Psalm 121:1–2).

"May the Lord answer you when you are in distress; may the name of the God of Jacob protect you. May He send you help" (Psalm 20:1–2).

"We wait in hope for the Lord, He is our help and our shield" (Psalm 33:20).

Most of the contexts are life and death, by the way, and God is your only hope. Your ezer. If He is not there beside you... you are dead. A better translation, therefore, of ezer would be "lifesaver." Kenegdo means alongside, or opposite to, a counterpart.

The thought that *ezer* could mean something like "lifesaver" was a far, far cry from my picture of wifedom. Then to read that *kenegdo* means "alongside, or opposite to, or counterpart," left me with so many questions. "Alongside" I could grasp easily enough. After all, it is how I viewed my role as a wife, to a degree. I was to be beside my husband, helping, supporting, encouraging, etc. But "opposite to" and even "counterpart," my mouth hung open as I pondered the fact that if the Creator used these words to define the purpose of a wife, I had so much more to learn. It was frustrating.

But I sighed as my shoulders relaxed a bit.

Realizing that we need to learn something can be comforting. It's the moment we rest knowing the missing pieces are about to come—since we've secretly known all along we needed something more. For all my efforts to be a good wife and mother, so many nights when I laid my head down to sleep (usually exhausted from trying so hard to be enough), I knew there was something important still missing.

Never Stop Learning

I read Captivating a second time and wondered at all I still needed to learn. Learning compels growth; growth compels learning. But life has a way of sweeping us up in its currents. Work demands our attention: groceries must be bought, dinners cooked, projects finished, children washed and tucked in safe at night. I needed more to be the more I knew I was not able to be.

Then several years later, I read Half the Church. Mentioned previously, this moving book again brought the words *ezer kenegdo* before me, this time more strongly. If you haven't read her book already, may I suggest your next read be Carolyn Custis

James' Half the Church (and go ahead and buy Captivating while you're there). James spends all of Chapter 5 unraveling the mystery of "The Ezer Unbound." This now was the second time in five decades this seeker had come across these words. Imagine it. I was a wife and realized I did not fully grasp the name given to me by the One who made me, understanding there was a clarification in the very words he used when he described the purpose for that first woman. I began to dig.

Learning compels growth; growth compels learning. (Yep, it's worth saying again.)

By this time, my children were in their 20s and no longer needed the focused attention required of a mother of toddlers and teens. Researching was common for us as Steve and I were embarking on new adventures daily.

Life's a comedy in a way, because just as quickly as you begin to think you've figured out how to saddle and ride a horse, the horse leaves, the car is invented, and you have to begin learning again. One season of life challenges us; we work hard figuring it out only to watch that season end and a whole new one blast through the door—sometimes knocking said door off its hinges.

Identity Trumps Roles... Every Time.

For Steve and me, this always meant more learning was needed, more growth. We began studying more intricately the roles of both husband and wife. We worked to get a handle on the fact that these "roles" were held fluidly (they altered greatly) based on the different cultures and beliefs of people around the world. When you live in different places, you begin to see how differently roles are viewed. But we were fascinated by the fact that identities were not fluid; they should not change. Roles change with the wind. Identities should not. Who we are should be fixed. It should remain intact no matter where we are living. But what we do easily changes.

All this opened our eyes to new rooms of learning.
- "Who" we are can strengthen "what" we do.
- "What" we do should not alter "who" we are.

You might be thinking, Well, of course... But for us, this was an epiphany that multiplied our ability to teach the truth of God's good plans for husbands, wives, and homes.

Our identity, for the Christian, is found when we look closely at who we are in Christ. Neil Anderson, author of one of our favorite books, aptly entitled Who I Am In Christ, does a solid job of opening eyes to the foundational need to know who we are according to the One who made us and the One who died to save us.

Who we are and what we do are two different things completely. What you do may change dramatically throughout your lifetime. You may be a teacher, doctor, mother, father, business owner, or stay-at-home parent. These roles are important. But they will change as the years go by. Who you are speaks more into the purposes and reasons for your life. What is your core belief? Who you are will help define how well (or poorly) you do what you do. The words "*ezer kenegdo*" speak more about who I am as a woman than what I do as a person. I came to realize that I had been basing my role as a wife and mother on what I did in the eyes of others (my husband, children, family, and friends), not who I was in God's eyes.

A woman can be a wife or not, a mother or not, a doctor or teacher or lawyer or seamstress or engineer. But if she understands that she was knit together for the core purpose of being an *ezer kenegdo*, she will begin to grasp the purpose she is equipped to bring to her different roles. Realizing the first woman was created for the first man and *ezer kenegdo* are the words GOD gave her, women must accept that our womanliness is infused with the same *ezer kenegdo* abilities.

Finding Yourself

I am a wife, mother, daughter, sister, teacher, writer, speaker, cook, and journeyer. My role as a wife has changed through the years. The needs of my children have changed as they have grown up. The ages of the students I've taught have ranged widely. For two decades I taught children younger than 10, and now I find myself teaching dear souls much older than my own children. I've taught on both sides of the world and in some places in-between. Even what I've taught and how I've taught have changed drastically based on the students, their needs, and the curriculum in front of me. Further still, how I speak or the way I write is altered by the audience I will be sharing with. The point is this: what I do has changed and it will continue to change. It should.

But who I am should not change. Who I am as I do each of these things must be grounded and sure, so that the way it is done is in line with my purpose in life and in line with the One who gives life. Therefore, there is a foundation underneath me that holds steadfast no matter what happens on top of it.

Several years ago, Steve and I invested a lot of time and money into the remodeling of our home. We made it better. It took time and hard work, but it was so much nicer after the work was done. We changed it, but in the end it was still home—same address, same resting place for our family.

Who I am does not change. I might improve by acquiring wisdom, knowledge, etc., but who I am at my core remains the same. What I do, where I go, or even how it is done might change based on improvements I've made in my practices or my responses to the needs around me. But who I am remains grounded on the purposes I have been created for.

Grasping this is crucial. Otherwise, we allow others to change us into what they need or want us to be. Instead, we must gain a good understanding of our identity so that we can shift in healthy ways during the seasons of life, always remaining who we are, but able to apply our identities in the different roles we hold. This means that when the children are fully independent in their adulthood (as they should become), the parents do not look around wondering, Who am I now? This means that when the lifetime missionary realizes her time in the field is complete, she doesn't return home wondering, Who am I? This means that the Olympic athlete does not have to wonder who he is when the knee blows or the shoulder goes and the speaking engagements end. Roles change, but the core of who we are only grows better if it's healthy and in line with our purpose for living, and these purposes should be defined by the One who gives us life.

What do roles and identities have to do with being an *ezer kenegdo*? Perhaps you're already in the boat with your oars in the water, headed down this new river of understanding. Being an *ezer kenegdo* is closely tied to every woman's identity. The *ezer kenegdo* is a big part of who she is and it will profoundly and beautifully impact what she does.

Specifically, this was God's "call" to every woman, and since God is the same yesterday, today, and forever, we can know without a doubt that it's still God's call to every woman today as well. May we grow in its understanding so we can raise our daughters to understand it more fully as they become the women God created them to be.

Chapter 5

The Kenegdo *More*

Dandelions are never planted. You never find them in a manicured garden. They grow where the winds carry them. Relentlessly, they grow. They are picked, pulled, dug up, and stepped on, but no matter how they are treated, they grow again. They know their purpose. They know their job. And with determination, they do it.

"It is not what I have done or what has been done to me that determines who I am. Rather it is who I am (in Christ) that determines what I do and how I live. My identity in Christ is not achieved; it's received. It is the unshakable ground upon which I build my life. I will not base my life upon what circumstances or others or even my own destructive thoughts say of me—but rather what God says about me." —Neil Anderson from *Victory Over the Darkness*

If you are a woman, one of the beautiful ways God defines you is by using two ancient words, two words that were seemingly tossed to the side in a garden long ago. But the Creator never dismissed the words, and even still today he is looking for those brave enough to live them out fully.

The One who created you longs for you to be his ezer kenegdo.

But let's be real about it...

Some skeptics, dare we say, many skeptics, might be thinking, *We never hear sermons about women being ezer kenegdos because the first one God created in the garden failed to live up to her calling. Therefore, isn't it obvious that if the first woman couldn't do it, then all women are doomed to fail at being ezer kenegdos? Why try? It was defeated in the garden.*

Can you hear the poison dripping from that kind of thinking?

Athletes working to better their games will practice long hours but still see moments of failure on the field. Does the coach yell at them to get off the field and never come back? No. Good coaches will reestablish the skills, techniques, and focus needed to continue growing the world-class athletes hidden inside the struggling young people in front of them.

Would the naysayer who says, "Eve failed in the garden, therefore, all women will fail at becoming the *ezer kenegdo*s God purposed them to be" also say the gold medalists should have give up years ago, after the first time they failed? It's a most important question, because there's a faint hissing sound in that way of thinking. It's the same deceitful hiss heard in the heads of future champions when they are down. It's a private, silent, toxic conversation that takes place only in their heads: *Stay down. Why get up? You'll only fail again. Why try?*

We love to watch those champions rise up, breathe deeply, and set their eyes like flint on the goal. We cheer! We feel it stir something in us! We want them to persevere against the whispers of defeat and grab hold of what is possible if they will just keep... pressing... ahead.

We can do it for athletes. Shouldn't we do it for the beautiful *ezer kenegdo*s who have been brought down time and time again in a world that uses, abuses, and accuses women of being weak, unable, subservient, and commodities meant only for the pleasure of men?

We cheer for the soldier, the athlete, and the rags-to-riches stories. We love that they rose above the challenges they faced and proved to everyone that with God all things are possible (Matthew 19:26). So, why do we look at Eve, and then look at women and say,

"They can't make it; the first one failed and, therefore, so will all others"?

It's a lie.

It's a scaly falsehood that hinders the daughter of God from being able to buckle the "belt of truth" around her (Ephesians 6:14). Please, can we stop it? If we allow that kind of toxic thinking to prevail, we choose to allow the confusion of the serpent's words and the death that came from his trickery to remain in our homes today. Can we open our eyes and see the God-intended gifts of the *ezer kenegdo*s around us and in us?

Turning on the Lights

When Thomas Edison was asked what he had to say about the thousands of times he failed when attempting to make the first light bulb, his response was, "I have not failed. I've just found 10,000 ways that won't work."

We *ezer kenegdo*s have this in common with Mr. Edison. We've seen countless examples of the many ways women have fallen short of the Creator's call on their lives. But may this writing compel us to rise above the dirt piled high upon us and keep us working toward the call on our lives.

We've opened up the meaning of *ezer* in the previous chapters, and we've touched on the meaning of *kenegdo*, but in this chapter we'll work to clarify the meaning of the original Hebrew word "*kenegdo*" and the fullness intended when the two words are used together.

Let's focus closely now on exactly what it means to be his *kenegdo*. It means to be "alongside or as in front of him," "opposite to or counterpart," "a warrior against evil attacking the home."

To Be Alongside or In Front of Him

God established this when he took from the man's side to form the woman. She is not to be beneath him, before him, behind him, or above him. She is rightly positioned beside him. Figuratively, we can see the husband's need for companionship met in this side-by-side way of living. Both the husband and the wife are image-bearers, carrying in them the image of the One who made them (Genesis 1:27). They are equal in the eyes of the One who created them (Galatians 3:28).

In her book *Half the Church*, Carolyn Custis James states:

> *"There is nothing second class about God's vision for his daughters, and the ezer holds the clues. For starters, kenegdo needs rehabilitating. "Suitable" can be taken a lot of different ways that don't do justice to the meaning of this word. Kenegdo indicates the ezer is the man's match— literally, "**as in front of him**"—as Ying is to Yang. I love how Victor Hamilton puts it: "[Kenegdo] suggests that what God creates for Adam will correspond to him. Thus the new creation will be neither a superior nor an inferior, but an equal. The creation of this helper will form one-half of a polarity and will be to man as the South Pole is to the North Pole" (emphasis added). **She will be***

*his strongest ally in pursing God's purposes and
his first roadblock when he veers off course."*

The picture this should bring to mind is given to us on the wedding day. In most marriage ceremonies, there comes a moment when the couple is asked to face each other. They are not in opposition at that moment. Rather, they are in front of each other for the purpose of being clear about whom each is addressing, whom each is marrying. This is vitally important on the wedding day. We want no confusion over who is marrying whom. It is equally important that they be in front of each other throughout their lives (figuratively). So often, with the passage of time, a couple gets so accustomed to each other, they inadvertently forget to hold each other in the important position of being "in front of." To assuage aloneness, Adam needed one that would be "in front of him," one that would know who he was and would be known by him.

Opposite or Counterpart?

The man and the woman are not the same. She can bear children; he cannot. But from his body comes the tiny swimming sperm that must find its way to the egg that comes from her body. Without both, no child can form. There is a lost beauty in understanding that they are opposite of each other and yet able to balance each other perfectly. They are vastly different and yet are created to be the perfect companion fit for the other. Even the physical fit between a man and a woman speaks of the perfect balance.

Consider the right hand and the left hand. They are formed to be a mirror image of each other, the same as the other, yet opposite. Together, they are able to accomplish much. They balance each other. Two right hands would be ill equipped to accomplish most physical jobs. A left hand must be used to counter the right. Try digging a hole with two right hands and no left. Imagine preparing a meal with two left hands but no right. The differences between men and women have long been fare for endless conversations and countless books. We think differently, process differently, nurture children differently, approach challenges differently. But when "who I am" (my identity) is in place, I am better able to bring my healthy, good portion to my half of the whole God intended for marriage.

The left hand and the right hand work perfectly together when lifting a heavy load. The left hand, however, will approach the load from a completely different side, completely opposite way, than the right hand. If each tries to lift from the same side, the load will never get off the ground. Instead, they will experience frustration over their inability to do the job.

Yet another way to look at it is by imagining an airplane. Picture the fuselage of the plane with one massive wing on each side. Those wings are opposite of each other. The husband will be one wing on the plane; the *ezer kenegdo* will be the other. She is in an equal, but opposite position. The wings are there to balance the plane, just as she is there to balance the home. Both wings rely on each other. But in truth, they are the exact opposite. Try to fly a plane with two left wings and nothing on the right side. It'll never make it off the ground.

Steve Shares:
The physics of how an airplane works is fascinating. How engineers are able to build and balance such a

large structure and create enough thrust to get one of those things into the air will always remain a mystery to me, yet I know that it works.

A friend was a Top Gun pilot for the U.S. Navy. Greg Stubbs has an interesting story of how his plane's physics were tested one day during practice. He has given me permission to share his story.

Greg and five of his comrades were performing air combat maneuvers just off the coast of Cape Hatteras. As the planes were approaching for the simulated engagement, his right wingman, focusing on the target, accidentally ran into Greg's F-18 at 500 mph, 25,000 feet above the Atlantic, ripping Greg's left wing in half and also taking off four to five feet of his tail wing. His plane was now facing downward, headed toward the ocean. Greg began testing his options to see if the plane was able to fly. By the grace of God and the skills he had learned, he was able to make the necessary compensations to fly back to the airfield and safely land what was left of his plane. Experts on the ground stated that what he had just done was not possible given the damage to his aircraft. His plane never flew again.

When we compare marriage to an airplane, we can see that the husband and wife represent the wings with God as the fuselage that holds them together. If one is "damaged" by sin, the marriage will begin to spiral downward in the direction of the one who has brought weakness into the marriage. Does it happen? Yes. When the damage comes, is it hopeless to continue? No, it's not, if you trust God and allow the Holy Spirit to maneuver you through the issues. Did Greg give up and hit the eject button? Thankfully, he did not,

but faced the problem that brought about a solution to restore his flight. Husbands and wives can do the same.

That's why it's vital that both husband and wife work to remain free from sin in order to maintain a level, balanced partnership in the home. That's why it's so important for a man to listen to his *ezer kenegdo* when she sees what he cannot. Like our friend Greg, once the damage has occurred, we have to work to regain and maintain a level flight.

A Warrior Against Evil

A woman can be a soft, nurturing presence in the home, but within seconds she can become a warrior when something or someone enters her home intending to wound those she cares for. When sharing these truths with groups, I ask, "What do you think would happen if you saw a mother walking in the park with her child and suddenly a wild animal or a violent person jumped from the bushes to attack the child?" Without fail there is a visible reaction from the women: eyes spark, shoulders tense, heads tilt, and they sit up a little straighter.

The answers come quickly, "She would fight!" "The mother would defend her child." "She would put herself between the attacker and the child." Even men in the room respond: "If she loves her child, she will fight to the death to save it." "The attacker will soon become the attacked." "The mother will fight for her child." Sadly, there are some cases where mothers do not protect their children. But these are the results of warped minds or twisted hearts. As a whole, worldwide, we know that mothers will protect their children.

This is a huge part of being an *ezer kenegdo*. The *kenegdo* portion of a woman's identity brings with it the warrior-like response inside every woman when she sees her home, her children, or even her husband in harm's way. God could have made the woman to have no more response than a wallflower when something wrong was taking place in the home. If he had, we would see it worldwide— women who did nothing to protect others. But that is not the case. Inside every woman is a warrior who will stand against anything intending to harm her family. For the daughter of God, this means she will be on guard against the presence of evil as well. She will be keenly aware when she feels "something isn't right. I can't quite put my finger on it, but I know something is wrong." And she will watch closely to determine what's not right so she can intervene and protect her home, her children, and her husband. The husband needs her to watch out for his home. Four eyes are better than two; it's a fortunate man who knows his wife will be watchful and attentive to the care of his children and home.

God's Word says the woman is the "weaker" vessel (1 Peter 3:7). This verse does not say she is weak, only that she is weaker. In our home, this is always true physically, usually true emotionally, and often true spiritually. It's a fact. Steve's shoulders can carry more, his heart can usually handle more, and in terms of spiritual pressures (and believe me, we've felt plenty of it living in the mission field and even writing this book), he is the one who is my solid rearguard, just as I am for him. Too many husbands have wrongfully looked at this verse and interpreted it to mean their wives were weak. Instead, we hope this *kenegdo* revelation will open eyes to see that the woman God made for man has a strength inside her that equips her to stand well and fight fiercely for the well-being of her home. What a gift this is in a world seemingly set on destroying homes.

"She will be his strongest ally in pursing God's purposes and his first roadblock when he veers off course" (from Carolyn Custis James above). What a needed help this warrior/partner is intended to be. She is created to be strong enough to stand beside him, with him, and for him—as an ally. She knows he will need an ally because there is an enemy lurking about looking to destroy the good plans of God for their home. She's not afraid. She's not weak and helpless. She's not so busy with her career or shopping with friends or even preparing dinner for the family that she's unaware of the important position she holds beside him—with him.

Not only should she be his strongest ally, she should also be his first accountability partner. Why? So that they together can stay steady at the plan and purpose God has called them to. The *ezer*'s position as "a roadblock to her husband when he veers off course" is not for the purpose of control or a show of power over him. It is for the purpose of unified success and protection. She wants what he wants, and they have agreed together to help each other achieve it.

For the home that has chosen to serve the Lord, each knows it will take the dedication of equally committed partners to accomplish it. Is it becoming clear that the degree of strength each brings is not nearly as important as the combined strength they can produce together? One modern-day picture of this can be seen in the ministry and lives of Billy and Ruth Bell Graham. They were unified in their ministry work. Each had different roles they agreed upon and shared responsibility for. But their individual identities and as a couple were wholeheartedly grounded in their love of God. They were a team. They were allies together and accountable to each other. If you read their books, you'll soon realize his strengths mingled with hers and hers with his until finally there was no line defining one from the other. She was for him; he was for her. They both were for God. They lived it out beautifully for the world to see.

Steve's Thoughts:

Men, from the beginning, we have been given the position to lead our homes, right? And we want to do it in a way that honors God, right? But have you lived long enough to realize that you need help in leading effectively? If you're honest, you will say yes. And if you did answer yes, how did you know you needed help? My answer would come from the long list of mistakes I've made when I tried to do it by myself.

A proud man will not admit he needs help in any circumstance. A proud man will drive miles beyond what is necessary just because he doesn't want to stop and ask for directions. A proud man will refuse to be told what to do or how to do anything beyond his own knowledge. This "pride" causes so much damage to the relationships around him and, more specifically, to the relationship with his wife. Why? What can be worth taking a chance to destroy a marriage and a relationship with God? The Bible speaks of a man's pride several times and its warnings against it. Wake up, men! Don't let pride destroy your life.

So how do you move from a prideful life to one of humility, allowing a teachable spirit to grow within you? Listen to those around you so that you can make

solid decisions for the ones you lead. And who did God put by your side to help you along the way? He blessed you with a wife to watch out for the things that you cannot see. We are not attuned to details the way a woman is. Admit it. Women see things that we don't. A wise man will tap into the very resource God gave him so that together they can reach the highest level of blessing in this life.

Don't forget that husbands and wives are to represent Christ and the church as witnesses to an unknowing world. Billy and Ruth Graham discovered the value of God's design for husband and wife early in their marriage and were a great example for us to follow. They allowed themselves to be held accountable to each other, which was proof of their humility. Humility pleases God. When we yield to one another, we are following Christ's example. Let me ask you, "Do you prefer being around someone who is prideful or someone who is humble?" Humility wins every time, but "pride comes before the fall." Show your gratefulness to God for the blessing of an *ezer* created just for you.

An article by William Sullik shares (with more technicality) his findings, as well as R. David Freedman's:

> The customary translation of the two words "ezer kenegdo" as helper-fit is almost certainly wrong. Recently, R. David Freedman has pointed out that **the Hebrew word ezer is a combination of two roots: -z-r, meaning "to rescue, to save," and g-z-r, meaning "to be strong."** The difference between the two is the first letter in Hebrew. Today that letter is silent in Hebrew; but in ancient times, it was a guttural sound formed in the back of the throat. The

"g" was a ghayyin, and it came to use the same Hebrew symbol as the other sound `ayin. But the fact that they were pronounced differently is clear from such place names, which preserve the "g" sound, such as Gaza or Gomorrah. Some Semitic languages distinguished between these two signs and others did not. For example, Ugaritic did make a distinction between the `ayin and the ghayyin; Hebrew did not. —R. David Freedman, "Woman, a Power Equal to a Man," Biblical Archaeology Review 9 [1983]:56–58).

It would appear that sometime around 1500 BC, these two signs began to be represented by one sign in Phoenician. Consequently, the two "phonemes" merged into one "grapheme." What had been two different roots merged into one, much as in English the one word "fast" can refer to a person's speed, abstinence from food, his or her slyness in a "fast deal," or the adamant way in which someone holds "fast" to positions. The case that begins to build is that we can be sure that `ezer means "strength" or "power" whenever it is used in parallelism with words for majesty or other words for power such as `oz or `uzzo. In fact, the presence of two names for one king, Azariah and Uzziah, both referring to God's strength, makes it abundantly clear that the root `ezer meaning "strength" was known in Hebrew.

Therefore, could we conclude that Genesis 2:18 be translated as "I will make a power [or strength] corresponding to man." Freedman even suggests on the basis of later Hebrew that the second word in the Hebrew expression found in this verse should be rendered equal to him. If so, then God makes for the man a woman fully his equal and fully his match. In this way, the man's loneliness will be assuaged.

The same line of reasoning occurs with the apostle

Paul, who urged in 1 Corinthians 11:10, "For this reason, a woman must have power [or authority] on her head [that is to say, invested in her]."

This line of reasoning, which stresses full equality, is continued in Genesis 2:23 where Adam says of Eve, "This is now bone of my bones and flesh of my flesh; she shall be called 'woman,' for she was taken out of man." The idiomatic sense of this phrase "bone of my bones" is a "very close relative" to "one of us" or in effect "our equal."

(taken from http://www.godswordtowomen.org/ezerkenegdo.htm)

Combining the Two Words IS the More

According to the quote above, the Hebrew word *ezer* is a combination of two roots: `-z-r, meaning "to rescue, to save," and g-z-r, meaning "to be strong." This one must be made very clear. The woman was not given to man to rescue or save him in the sense that he was weaker and in need of her valiant help. Some have falsely implied this in an effort to elevate themselves. Instead, this is more appropriately explained with regards to Adam's aloneness. It was not good for man to be alone—the woman would rescue or save the man from that sense of aloneness. Secondly, the woman was not made to be weak. She was taken from Adam's side. Therefore, she has a semblance of his strength in her, but she carries it differently. She is made to be strong, but this does not imply a strength that should be compared to Adam's. Realistically, do two soldiers in battle pause to compare who is stronger than the other?

We hope not. If they do, they will both be beaten. Instead, two soldiers on a battlefield work to ebb and flow their efforts beside each other. One will react and respond as needed to correspond with the strength of the one beside him. They will work to apply each of their abilities in ways that will complement the other's abilities. Therefore, they accomplish a greater strength unified than either of them would have had alone. The very word *ezer* implies that a woman will be a strong helper.

Ezer *kenegdo* was the clarifying name given by the Creator. It was meant to enable her to know "who" she was created to be. When God looked at man (Adam) and said it was not good for him to be alone, he knew the man he created needed a partner, a counterpart, someone who would work opposite of him (not in opposition to him), someone who would have a warrior strength, who would stand beside him for the purposes of good. Without this *ezer kenegdo*, the man would be alone when trying to face the many challenges that God knew would come to him—both in the perfect Garden of Eden and in the world that was soon to come.

Chapter 6

His Half – Her Half – Our Flop

Every dandelion blossom boasts an average of 150 individual petals. Each petal is strategically placed beside the others, and all together they form a perfect circle, mimicking the sun above them. One petal alone can never accomplish the full circle the flower is intended to portray. Each petal must do its part.

Getting Personal

How is it possible to spend so many years working to be the submissive, prayerful, organized, tidy, support-him wife and yet miss the mark in such profoundly important ways? There are a million ways to miss a target. Thomas Edison found 10,000 ways, and I have surely surpassed him in this. Failure is only failure when we give up. Success is found in trying again.

I had sat in church and taken notes. I had asked questions and read the books. But during the first three decades of our marriage, Steve and I knew we were missing the key to a buried treasure that lay somewhere between us.

While I had been learning about being a submissive wife (Ephesians 5:22, 24; Colossians 3:18), I had also been learning about the headship role of a husband in his home (Ephesians 5:23; 1 Corinthians 11:3). It looked like a challenging but right fit. Steve was to be the head of our home and I was to submit to him. He was also supposed to love me and I was to respect him (Ephesians 5:22–33)—all good things. For all these teachings we have the utmost respect, and Steve and I dedicated ourselves to forging our home in these ways. But we sensed something was still amiss. And it was.

> **To bring more clarity, Steve shares:**
> **"What does it mean to be the head of your home? When Donna and I married, I had no clue. So for a while, I just let her make most of the decisions. Donna is a lively, creative thinker who always comes up with good ideas, so it was much easier for me to follow her rather than put the effort and energy into leading our**

home. I wasn't doing my part. We were two people who loved each other and were trying to do the best we could, not really knowing the roles we were called to fill, roles that had been commissioned by our Creator.

"In a conversation we had early in our marriage, Donna said to me, 'You are supposed to be the head of our home. You are the one who is to lead us.' It scared me because I didn't know how to do that. It had not been modeled in the home I grew up in, not the way the Bible teaches. My parents were good people who taught me how to be respectful of others, the importance of knowing Christ, working hard, and things like that, but how to lead my home was not one of them. It felt as though I had been shoved out on a stage under bright lights with no script or acting ability, unable to perform."

Donna: Without understanding my identity, much less my role (having never heard of *ezer kenegdo*), I had wrongly adopted the submissive, subservient attitude in our home: you lead, I'll follow; you decide, I'll comply; you are responsible; I'll get dinner on the table. And Steve felt pushed out onto the platform—alone. (I wonder if sometimes it felt more like "walking the plank"?)

As Steve has often put it: "One of the wheels on our cart just kept popping off."

He was frustrated over the demands I placed on him. And what's more, I had the Bible backing me up. It's just the worst thing ever when someone uses the Bible to make a point in an argument. Just awful! He was, in fact, to be the head of our home. But I was frustrated because I had placed a restriction on myself. I was not to "lead." He had to, I was to submit and help him (whatever that meant). We were like two mules yoked side by side in marriage but pulling in different directions. We were banging into each other as we desperately tried to fill our "roles." We didn't understand "who" we were. We thought what we were supposed to do would bring about the definition of "who" we were supposed to be. There they are... roles (what we do) and identity (who we are). So, the wheel kept falling off our cart—about once or twice a month.

Slowly, though, the light came on as our children got older and I finally forced myself to face the challenges of role vs. identity. I'd focused so much of my energy on raising our children and trying to be a good wife to Steve that when the children didn't need me as much, I began wondering if I was a necessary part of our home. I'd done my best, but it seemed I was quickly being left behind— even by Steve. This was not his doing; it was mine. In many ways our marriage was wonderful. We worked hard to bless each other and those around us. This lost piece was not obvious and it didn't hamper our ability to accomplish valuable things in other areas of our lives. But we knew that we still had more to learn. And if we did not stay steady in the pursuit of it, we would not arrive at the place we both wanted to be in our relationship.

Wherever You Go, You'll Still Find You.

This journeying continued for many years. And then God called us to move to Kenya to serve full-time ministering to marriages and families. *What, Lord? You want us, as imperfect as we are, to serve you where and how?* God made it clear to us exactly what HE was calling us to do. Truthfully, our knees shook. We knew we were still learners, so how could we be the best choice? But obedience is obedience, and we didn't want to end up in the belly of a big fish.

We moved to Kenya. Steve loved it. I was struggling intensely over the loss of hearth and home and family around me. My role and my identity were enmeshed still, but I honestly was not aware of it. God was about to take me through the process of finally, completely separating the two and he knew he could best do that when all my comforts were removed. He knew it was going to be a painful process. But it was his love that wanted me to know who I was in his eyes.

Many around us had no idea of the learning curve we were trying to ride. Truthfully, in most areas of our lives, we had all the ducks in a row (well, if they weren't in a row, they were at least in the right ponds).

Years before, I had read Anderson's aforementioned book Who I Am In Christ and fully believed I held my identity in Christ. But when the birds flew from the nest and the one I'd made the nest with was thriving as I was shrinking, we both realized that I was floundering. All the years I'd been saying, "I'll pray for you; you decide" had brought us to a place of... Steve had been forced to deal with many things apart from my position of balancing our home (it is possible to be overly submissive ladies), and now when I wanted to be included in the partnership, we both realized we had been working out of alignment. No wonder that wheel kept popping off all those years.

I had become too weak. Steve had become too strong.

Again, we really were thriving in other areas of our lives, but this roller coaster was taking us both on a ride we didn't want to continue. We didn't want to leave each other. Our love and commitment was still strong toward each other and God. But we just didn't want to be "who" we had become toward each other.

Here's the ugly of how it looked. A challenge would come to us. Steve might ask my thoughts, or he might not. I (having no children to manage) would over-zealously form my thoughts and work to interject my opinions. He would wonder about my newfound enthusiasm. The decision would be made, but I would be left with a sense of "he is tolerating me" rather than "he is valuing me." I would ask him about it, and he would wonder how to handle me. I'd be hurt. He'd get upset. I'd be more hurt. He'd get angry. We'd both blow up. And aloneness would smother us. Aloneness. The very thing God said it was not good for Adam to feel, the very thing our marriage should not be feeling after so many years. There it was. Aloneness. Can you hear the faint hiss of that scaly, on-the-job serpent?

Pulling Back the Veil, Nothing Hidden

Here are some words from Steve to bring even more understanding to this strange place we found ourselves in.

> **Steve shares:**
> **"So how did we get to this place? How does any couple find themselves alone, even when we are looking right at each other? For us, it had everything to do with my selfishness, and being selfish comes in many forms. Mine was cleverly disguised in a kind of false humility. It was so undercover that neither Donna**

nor I could see it until we read it in a book. In Tim LaHaye's book Spirit-Controlled Temperament, he explained how a phlegmatic personality, which is me, is typically selfish. I was the one reading out loud that day and asked Donna, "Would you say that I am selfish?" She answered, "No. I haven't thought of you as being selfish until you just now read it in the book." I quickly agreed having never been able to see my own selfishness because of its passive-aggressive nature in me.

"I say all this to bring to light the fact that my responses (or lack of responses) toward Donna were rooted in self-based, subconscious thinking. Can you see it? I was even so lazy that I didn't invest any time in thinking about these things enough to realize what was going on inside of me, which made me feel bad about myself, which is a selfish way of thinking! May I be so bold as to say that many men do the same. Mark Gungor, famous author, speaker, and personality expert, talks about how women think on multiple levels and speeds while men prefer to think in one "box" at a time. I'm that guy! And that's what was happening in our marriage to bring us both to the place of aloneness."

Our response to it: we struggled and asked for help from many. While reading one day, the Father brought me back to the words he spoke in the beginning. I was reminded of his call to me to be an *ezer kenegdo*, and I knew it was his guidance to begin the hard work of redoing, remodeling, tearing out the old, and letting him make this new. After much conversation, tears, confessions, and prayers for each other, we began a new journey.

We would relearn the truths of my role and his. We'd recommit ourselves to the identities we are called to have in Christ. No more confusion, but rather a full embracing of God's call for a wife, an *ezer kenegdo*, Steve's helper that is equal to him, a fellow image-bearer, the opposite part of the whole we would make together. No more so subservient that he feels as if he must stand alone, and I am left wondering if my part counts.

Aligning the Head with the Ezer

Of the many women I've been privileged to share life with, they all have a gleam in their eyes and a quick nod to their heads when we begin talking about their inner strength. When the words "warrior strength standing against evil in her home" are used, women lean forward and smile. Why? They feel strength inside them, but they've never really known what to do with it. If misplaced, this strength can oftentimes lead to striving and struggling with their husbands or children/teenagers or sisters or mothers or neighbors or friends.

Women can be strong. Some women are even fierce! If you spend a little time in Kenya, you'll be amazed at the strength in the women there. But it's true for women everywhere. As shared in the previous chapter, God gave his girls a strength that he wanted them to use for very careful and specific reasons. He wants his image-bearing daughters to stand against evil, against what is wrong, against what will wound their homes. Rightly used, this strength crafts a home into a haven. A wounded child can rest safely under its cover. A husband under attack from the world around him can find peace and renewed confidence beside an *ezer kenegdo* willing to use her strength for the right reasons.

She's still "weaker" than her husband, but she's gifted with the ability to be strong in ways that can shock them both—if she understands it and uses it in the right ways.

Oddly, it can sound like hidden super-woman strength. In some ways, it actually is. But if it's not appreciated and grown, it can fade away and die, leaving her home off-balance. Likewise, if it's not handled in God-honoring ways, it can wound her home and do the opposite of what it was intended to do. *Ezer kenegdo* beauty is seen when the struggles of this world try to penetrate the home, but she stands firmly for what is good and sets the stage for what is right to win. The husband has his very important position—the headship of the home. A greater strength is given to him to be the strong arm of protection, provision, and cover for his wife and family. We've seen it so often when challenges have come.

He is stronger.

But, the *ezer kenegdo* piece has become so crucial for our marriage because so often Steve will be focusing on several different very important matters. But, honestly, who can focus on everything all at once? So, because of the good focus he has on some things, other things could be slipping past his radar. Thankfully, he has a co-pilot, a sidekick, a partner beside him who is not focusing on the same things he is, and is, therefore, better able to notice the things that otherwise would have gotten by him, by us, and, most likely, left some area of our home limping. A man needs a strong woman beside him in this world.

Steve's thoughts here:
"When we learn of a new concept, a new word, or something profound that has never been taught or

even mentioned, it creates a curiosity in us to learn more for the purpose of validation or elimination. This is especially true when it directly affects the way we think or how we live. This is what happened to our home when the "*ezer*" word was first introduced. I don't wish to rewrite what Donna has already explained, but I do want to support what she is saying. It is also in support of what God had intended from the beginning. His perfect design was for a man to be a strong leader, filled with compassion and kindness. He was to be wise and innocent. I love a line from one of my favorite movies called Robin & Marian. It is the Robin Hood story 20 years after, when old Robin returns from the Crusades with Little John still by his side. After a battle with his life-long rival, the Sheriff of Nottingham, Robin speaks to Marian of Little John's bravery by saying, "Did you see John on the field? No one is more gentle, nor half as terrible." This is one of the highest compliments the male ego could ever receive. And isn't that what we should be, men? Gentle and fierce all for the right reasons and pointed in the right direction?

A good example of an *ezer kenegdo* is portrayed in another movie, 300. King Leonidas is a strong leader with great compassion for his people and beside him stands his queen, Gorgo. One of the early scenes finds Leonidas needing to make an important decision that will change the course of his kingdom. When threatened by a potential enemy, the king turns to his wife for guidance, which came in a gentle nod to which he responded in agreement. Had she signaled her husband to change the course, he would have listened. He valued her input as important and that his decision alone would have been based on his charged emotions, leading them in the wrong direction.

In the book of Matthew, we read that Pontius Pilate was face with the fate of Jesus. As he sat in the judgement seat, not knowing what to do, Pilot's wife, his ezer, "sent him a note warning him not to have anything to do with this innocent man." (Matthew 27:19) She did this for the purpose of protecting her husband. She was not trying to rule over him or to govern the governor. Ultimately, Pilate did not listen to his wife and therefore he handed Christ over to the people who crucified him. When Pilate chose not to listen to the ezer God had given him, he made the biggest mistake of his life.

When I married Donna, she hoped for a knight in shining armor. I wanted to be a King Leonidas or a Little John in our home, making all the right decisions that would benefit our family. We learned that God speaks to us both so that pride will not overtake either. It is a wise man who listens when his wife speaks and an even wiser man who thinks to ask her opinion and include her in decision-making.

A man needs a strong woman to see the things he is not able to see. A man needs a woman who will open her mouth so that they will finish strong together."

Carolyn Custis James – from Half the Church: "Descriptions of the woman as dependent, needy, vulnerable, deferential, helpless, leaderless, or weak are—to put it simply—wrong. The ezer is a warrior."

Redeemed Love Wins

So how did it turn out for us? Did we make it? You wouldn't be holding this book if we had caved in and given up. What we can say about the truths we are sharing with you here is that a woman must understand who she is before she can rightly love herself or love another. For us, we've dug deeply into that first garden looking for seeds of truth. And it's brought us to a new place, a new garden, a new love that is deeper, richer, and more right than we ever dreamed possible. We've had to fight for it, but we no longer have to fight each other over it.

Falling in love is easy and sweet. Staying in love is hard work. Redeemed love is the most beautiful of all. God's way works.

—————— Chapter 7 ——————

The Two Become One, Because...

The dandelion stem produces natural latex containing the same qualities as the rubber found in rubber trees. Companies are currently testing its strength and finding it may very well be the next bonding element in tires. Combined with other materials, this tiny flower's latex has the strength of what has previously only been found in a tree.

Question Marks

Imagine how Peter and Andrew felt that day long ago on the shores of Galilee. They were doing what they'd been taught to do: throw the nets into the water, haul in the fish. The same was true for James and John, sons of Zebedee. It was a normal sunny day and the fish were there for the catching. They knew what to do.

Then Jesus called to them, "Come, follow me, and I will show you how to fish for people!" (Matthew 4:18–22)

Without a doubt, there were invisible question marks over their heads. *What? You want us to do what? But don't you see, we are fishermen... who fish... for fish?*

And yet there was holiness to the call that lured them away from the comfort of what they knew and called them into places they never dreamed they would be found doing things they never imagined possible. Do you see them? Question marks over their heads? We do.

Those same question marks found us as well. And when the One who made you calls you, there's a birth of HOPE that what you know you cannot do, he will do, and you will be HIS WITNESS. We laid down our "nets" and followed. Our parents became modern-day Zebedees.

We never planned to become that couple that cared for other couples. But the One who made us steadily worked it into our lives. So imagine how surprised we were when our own limping pains carried us to the Father for healing, which then brought others to our front porch with similar limping pains. When you've faced walls and learned how to climb over them, it's beautiful how it grows your desire to help others over their walls. When God shows up in your own life, you know it's way too much to try to keep to yourself. He is a double-portion Father. So when he gives, it compels us to give too.

And there's humility in the journey.

The smell of "fish" on the hands of fishermen was slowly replaced with the aroma of the Father—the One who takes fishermen and makes them disciples, who takes a couple and makes them his own.

We've shared with every couple we've ever ministered to that we do not have a perfect marriage. Goodness, we have hurt each other so much. But, we do have a deep desire to hold on for the ride, learn all we can, believe God, and prove his Word is true. And, oddly-wonderfully enough, with our commitment to God and each other, we've learned more about who we are (individually and together), who he is, what he says, and how he works.

And therein lies the holy grail of marriage (are we allowed to say it that way?).

Exactly What Is the Purpose of Marriage?

Marriage is a physical representation of Christ and the church. The husband is to love his wife like Christ loves the church... and gave himself up for it (Ephesians 5:25). Wives are to submit to their husbands just as the church is to submit to Christ (v. 24) and support the husband as the head of the home just as Christ is the head of the church (v. 23).

Marriage matters so much to God. Never once does he tell us it's going to be easy or even fun (although it certainly can be). God knows we are going to face hard days, and he wants us to have someone b-e-s-i-d-e us. We don't have to face the hard days alone. A man loving his wife and caring for her, a wife being a submissive *ezer kenegdo* (a helper that stands beside him with a strength of a warrior opposing evil but submitted under the godly leadership of her husband) can overcome much. Is it beginning to make sense?

We were created for relationship. We need it.

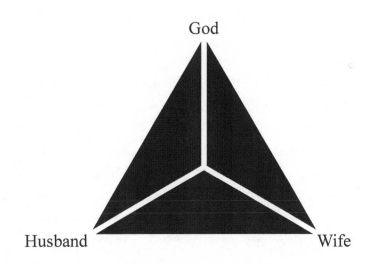

This creates the triangle connecting us together. As our "vertical" ascends toward God, we grow closer to each other.

Within the beautiful plan of marriage, God desires to increase both the vertical and the horizontal quality of relationships. When a husband and wife share their lives, there should be a comfort as aloneness is defeated in this horizontal (side-by-side) relationship. We are not talking about the sexual union. We are speaking of the heart-to-heart, emotional friendship. The sexual union is beautiful and it does matter greatly, but the horizontal relationship we are speaking of is that part of us that shares life and laughter and tears and pain with another person. It's what Jesus was wanting the night he prayed in Gethsemane when he asked the three disciples to go with him to the garden and pray for him. He did not want to "feel alone." Even Jesus longed for those life-giving horizontal connections found in emotional friendships.

As couples journey through life together, they will come upon obstacles and they both will realize that they need help getting past these challenges. **We did.**

We knew that to climb the mountains we encountered in our marriage, we needed help. So where did we go? We went to GOD. We knew we needed his help, his guidance, and the truth of his Word. We also went to mentors, to those we'd noticed living in a way that spoke of the "more" we knew we needed. Pride had to go. We needed help. It was not the time to act like everything was fine; it was time to be honest, to admit that we were broken, and to seek godly guidance from those who had felt his touch in their marriages. Being mentored by a couple that clings to God is just one more way of going to God for help. And yes, we sought guidance from good Christian counselors as well.

And what happened then? The vertical relationship increased.

What? You mean the vertical relationship increased BEFORE the horizontal relationship changed? Yes. We knew that for our marriage to survive and thrive, we needed more of the One who created marriage in the first place. No other religion can do this. No mini-god is able. Only the ONE who created us for the purpose of relationship with each other and with him could have woven together such a beautiful way of growing us—vertically and horizontally.

Imagine it. Wallow in it.

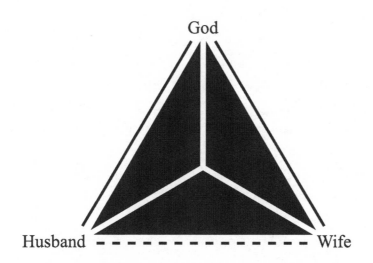

Our marriages are designed to increase our relationships with one other person (our spouse) and the one holy God.

Because She Matters

Recently I enjoyed a cup of tea with a young man who loves his wife very much. As the conversation unfolded, he shared that he knew there was "more" for them, but he couldn't quite figure out how to get to it. No one was being unfaithful; no one was leaving. But after several years of marriage, they'd become successful in some ways but lacking in others, and they wondered what was missing.

They had the nice house, nice cars, good jobs. They had their health, family, friends, hobbies, and pets. They went to church on Sundays and tried to do the right things in life. But something was "off." Since I'd known this young man for many years, I had a sense of the love and sincerity of heart they held for each other. So I asked him, "Do you pray for your wife every day?" He looked down and said, "Well, I definitely pray for her, but I wouldn't say I pray for her every day." I asked, "When you were pursuing your educational degrees, and you came to a big examination day, did you pray then?" "Yes!" he said. "I wouldn't have had the courage to mark the first answer before asking God to help me." I shared, "So, when it came to taking the test, you knew you needed God's help, right?" "Yes!" "But when it comes to living beside your wife, you can too often think you don't need God's help... as if loving and caring for another person means giving her what she wants and getting what you want from her. And if you can just keep that scale of give and get balanced, then you'll be *happy*."

He smiled and looked down. I reminded him of the serpent in the garden and we talked about the timing of that serpent's arrival just after the woman (the gift), the one designed to solve Adam's problem of aloneness, had been given to him. And then I shared, "If the serpent showed up just in the nick of time to put a kink in the horizontal relationship between the woman and the man (not working together well), but then also the vertical relationship between God and them (doubting God's instructions), why do we think he's not still lurking around hoping we won't notice him?"

If we need God to help us think clearly on test day, don't we need God to help us think clearly as we love the one beside us? Every day? We all know tests can be retaken. Scores in the classroom can be improved. It takes hard work and prayer. But do we overlook the importance of the daily score we receive from the one person we have chosen to share the rest of our lives with? Isn't that daily score much, much more important in the wide-angle view of life?

Conversation was rich at the realization that the lurking serpent was not dead. Just because we can't physically hear him hissing nearby doesn't mean we can naively believe all is well and we don't need God's help in our homes every day.

The first home came under serious attack... as does every home from then until now.

The enemy of our Lord does not want the gift of relationship to survive. He knows if he can make us feel alone, he can drag us into a pit (mentally) and weaken our ability to believe the Father loves us and wants us to love one another. This wonderful young husband got it! His eyes began to twinkle as he embraced this first step in moving toward the "more" his Father had for both his wife and him—prayer, daily prayer, praying for God's help in the good work of loving his wife well. There are more steps to come, but strengthening the vertical relationship (through prayer) for the horizontal relationship (with his wife) would begin.

It's About His Love

Steve and I love each other. That's for sure. But we know, and we hope you know, that love in a marriage is not enough. Love is a choice between a man and a woman. Love can be soft and warm, but it can also be tough and challenging. Love matters. Love covers, comforts, cares, carries, and confides. Love is wonderful when it's up close, when it comes near. Love becomes fragile when there's too much distance between two hearts. When the serpent starts talking as he did in the garden, love can flounder and, given enough time, it can begin to doubt, accuse, hide, betray, and deny. It takes more than flesh-covered love.

Our roles in marriage will be successful only to the degree that we are willing to let the Creator give us the identity he made us for, never forgetting that it's "who" we are that will then enable us to best do "what" we are called to do. The who and the what are completely separate. Who we are can strengthen what we do, but what we do does not change who we are. Those words are revisiting us here from Chapter 4, because they fit here perfectly as well.

It might seem as though I'm chasing a rabbit down a trail and getting off course from the title of this chapter. I'm not. I promise. It's a near impossibility for "two to become one" if the individuals don't have a clue about who they are. It's a way the enemy works to destroy a marriage before it even begins. He revels at the chance to confuse us about "who" we are, so we're then confused about "how" to love. If he can keep us focused on what we do and/or on what our spouses do, then we'll miss who each other is. Knowing who we are is vital individually, but in marriage too! Dr. Seuss might have said it this way: "A 'who' can love better, but a 'what' cannot" (gotta have a little fun sometimes).

We are God's first. That's our identity. That is whose we are—HIS. God made us because he, the Creator, desires to have a relationship with us. Why? Because he loves us. God's love for you is not based on what you do (or don't do).

It's really about God's love for you. Marriage is just one of the ways God wants his love to flow through us to another. Spiritual intimacy—the miracle love that flows between God and the two souls he has made into one. He's such a God of love that he creates souls and places them in people in order to have places from which his love can flow. It's that artesian well effect again. He, God, is a constant gush of love looking for tributaries to carry him far. The most broken among us rarely realize how deeply and completely they are loved by the One who made them. Those broken and wounded in marriage are perhaps the most devastated of all, for they have a knowing deep inside that they've missed something that should have been, could have been, if only it had been... beautiful.

Because Vertical Relationship Makes All the Difference

God is love. He gives love. He designs people to need love and places within them the ability to give love as well. He wants love in marriage. He knows marriages will survive and thrive if their love lines connect—horizontally (with others) and vertically (with him).

This horizontal and vertical love can certainly flow for all people, married or not. Love is found in many relationships. But the uniqueness of the horizontal and vertical love in marriage is that when a husband and wife are joined together, they become one (Gen. 2:24).

Therefore, the husband and wife have the chance to have a profound connection with God within the marriage. The husband and wife should always maintain their individual relationship with God. It's a must for personal, healthy growth. But in marriage, they are also able to connect vertically with God in their "oneness." *It's a whole new level of intimacy.*

Here's an example that can clarify.

When Steve wakes up in the morning, he heads to his office. He grabs a cup of coffee and spends time with God reading, praying, writing, etc. A little while later, I wake up and say my morning prayers for family and friends before my feet ever touch the floor. Around 6:00 a.m., dear Steve brings me a cup of coffee (yes, in bed), and I open my Bible and have my quiet time. Steve goes back to his office, and I remain in our room. We are each connecting individually with our Father.

Then we navigate (it's a natural sort of happening that comes after years of reading each other's morning movements) toward the den or front porch. We sit and talk, often either about what we read or something we learned or for someone we're praying for. Then we usually read something together. It doesn't have to be long, but it matters to us that we are learning something new together. Then we pray together.

We individually have a vertical connection with God. We have a horizontal connection with each other (talking and reading together). And finally we have another vertical and horizontal connection as we pray together (it's the two-are-one part).

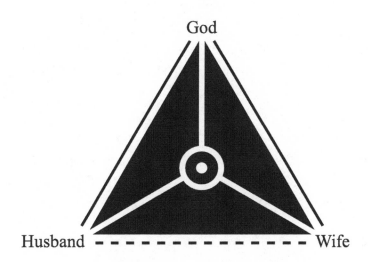

Does that seem odd? I sure hope not. Because in the middle of all those "connections," God comes near, and we are better able to care for each other and the world around us.

As we began sharing this with other couples, we realized there were very few couples that were connecting in these amazingly simple, but life-changing ways. Some husbands or wives might have their own personal times with God. Others aren't even doing that. But most don't consider the second way they could connect with the Father and each other at the same time.

Never Give Up. Never Stop.

It's one of the ways an *ezer kenegdo* will care for her home and protect it. Pray. Pray for her husband and children. But it doesn't end there. An *ezer kenegdo* looks further than the physical needs of her home. She is willing to step into the spiritual places of lack and recognize the needs. It's not easy, but it's vitally important. Her home needs to be helped with a strength that reflects her willingness to use her warrior heart and stand in opposition to anything that would wound or destroy those in her home.

We can bake the most magnificent meals and decorate our homes exquisitely, but if that home is not guarded against the ever-working serpent and grown in the ways of "As for me and my house, we will serve the Lord" (Joshua 24:15), then it's only a matter of time before decay sets in.

Steve Shares:
A long time back, when Donna and I realized our "connections" with each other were primarily in the emotional and physical areas, we knew something was missing. There had to be more. Our emotional connection began as friends before we ever dated. That connection continued into marriage and so came the physical connection. These two ways of communicating with each other are quite common in most marriages, or at least they begin that way. When we were wisely asked the question if we were enjoying a spiritual connection, we said yes. We prayed for meals; we each read the Bible; we prayed for each other and our children; and we went to church and tithed. Yes, we were spiritually connected.

I was satisfied, but, thankfully, my *ezer kenegdo* was

not. As Donna began to ask questions of older, godly women, she was hearing that there was more—the more she had felt was missing, but didn't know what it was or how to find it. So Donna came to me to talk about how we could get to the more. One of the ways was to pray with each other. *Me? How can I do that?* shot through my mind. The enemy of our Lord was paying close attention to what was about to happen in our home and was not about to let it come easily. I feared speaking out loud in front of Donna because in my mind, she was more educated than I was; she knew the Bible better than I did; she was more spiritual than I have ever been; and I will sound like a fool—which is pride in the rough. I will disappoint her. How can we reach this new connection?

I will never forget her tender words of encouragement to me, "Honey, I don't care what you say, how much you say, or how it will sound. What I will hear is my husband, the leader of my home, speaking to my heavenly Father about me and our children and that will bring the love and security that I/we need. So, please, let's begin living this way." And we did.

As time passed, the words came more easily and more abundantly with a confidence that can only come from Christ and our obedience to him. This was the *ezer* in Donna at work.

While raising three children, working at our jobs, and maintaining a house, how could we find the time to make this a part of our daily worship? For me, it began early in the mornings. There is no better time, I will say, than before everything wakes up and before the demands of the day sweep us away. Donna once read that Mother Teresa was quoted saying, "I have so much to do today, it will take at least three to four hours of prayer to prepare for it." I will never be in the same league as that precious saint, but from that point, my days began, as Donna mentioned, with a cup of hot coffee and the Lord. And before I would leave for work, Donna and I would pray with and for each other. Oh, how it blessed us. We have no idea what our Father has for us until we are still before him. We have no idea the difference it will make in our homes and our families until we take that step. Our family reaped the goodness of God.

To go further, Donna came to me again with an urging from the Holy Spirit that I begin to pray with our children. The time with my kids was limited with work and school, so it was the perfect way to connect with them just before they went to sleep. For small children, that can be an intimidating way to end the day, being left alone in their dark rooms expected to rest when they are at their most vulnerable. So it began, one child at a time, asking about their days and what their prayer needs were. It was such a rich investment into the lives of our little people. Did they respond? Oh, how they responded in such beautiful, godly, childlike ways. I wouldn't trade those nights with my kids for anything.

And I have my *ezer kenegdo* to thank for it. It was her connection to the Father that led me to this blessing. I have not been an easily convinced man for Donna to live with, but when I have listened and followed through with what the Holy Spirit was saying through her, the blessings did and do flow.

We practice who we really are first with those who live closest to us... our spouses, children, etc. Then, as we grow, it begins to overflow into what we do both in and outside the home. This is authentic living from the inside out. Too often we confuse this process by trying to be something impressive outside the home. But when we walk through the door at the end of the day, we morph into a less-careful version of ourselves that mows the grass or cooks dinner or just sits on the couch to watch fake lives on the screens in front of us. These are dangerous symptoms of people who don't actually know (or live out) WHO they are. Instead, they get stuck on the treadmill of what they DO.

Let's pause and ponder the truth here and have the courage to realign what might have gotten knocked off course.

The great hope of "two becoming one flesh" is when each of the two knows who he or she is and is willing to carry their own half of the whole for the benefit of others.

Chapter 8

The Wide Pendulum Swing

Dandelions head the list of excellent foods for the liver. This herb has been used for centuries to treat jaundice and the yellowing of the skin that comes with liver dysfunction, cirrhosis, and hepatitis. It is used to detoxify the liver and reduce the side effects of prescription medications. Used correctly, the dandelion brings health and healing to the liver, the part of the human body given the task of filtering blood, detoxifying chemicals, and metabolizing medications. The dandelion has much to offer. But if it is never used for these good purposes, its value lays dormant and all it could have accomplished is never realized.

What's That Smell?

Years ago, in the BC (before children) days of our marriage, we took a vacation with my sister and brother-in-law. Driving separate cars, we caravanned our way to the beach... blue skies above, blue waters ahead. The highway stretched before us. The windows were down and the music was loud. We stopped at a restaurant south of Atlanta and then got back on the road and headed into the sunset.

We covered the miles quickly—wind in our hair, salt water on our minds. A couple of hours south of Macon, Georgia, we made a pit stop. My sister and I dashed in for snacks, while the guys pumped gas. When we came back, I noticed flies all around Steve's legs. As he swatted flies, he looked down and noticed something black on his shoe, and leg, and sock, and knee. It was dog-poop! He quickly looked in the Jeep and, yep, there it was, all over the floorboard where he had been sitting. He realized he must have stepped in it outside the restaurant a few hundred miles back. He had unknowingly smeared it everywhere, but only now realized it because of the flies and the smell.

It was terrible! Since we'd been driving with the top off the Jeep, we hadn't smelled it in the open air. But now, there it was.

What an odd way to begin a chapter, right? But hold on. It actually applies. We had no idea what was there on Steve's shoes. We were oblivious to it. Our minds were on the coast ahead of us, not on the mess stuck to us. We all come to places in our lives when we begin to realize that something stinks! The wind's not blowing the smell away. Instead, we find ourselves standing in stagnant air realizing we've been living with "that" in our lives all this time. We'd been so focused on other things, we hadn't even noticed the "smell." We'd been so focused on our own feelings, we hadn't noticed the truth of the hurt, the loneliness, the distance we had caused. And what's worse, we realize others around us probably knew it was there all along.

For good or for evil, we all get to choose.

This chapter asks us to get real with God and ask him, "Is something smelling that I need to clean up, Lord?"

If you're not married yet, this chapter could be good preventative medicine, if you'll let it sink in. If you are married, it will hopefully compel you to carefully check your heart and actions. This chapter won't be comfortable for those who have been thinking they've been "right," but silently keep wondering at the nagging feeling in their guts that something was wrong. This is that dreaded introspective chapter, the one that says, "Look in the mirror and let God show us what we need to see from his heart."

Remembering that all women were created to be *ezer kenegdo*s, we must realize that just because we were created for something doesn't mean we will automatically live out that calling. Consider the person born with an amazing ability to hold steady under intense pressure. This person might choose to use that skill to become a sniper in the armed forces. He knows his ability and he chooses to use it for the benefit of his government forces to stand against those intending harm to many.

One effective sniper can save the lives of hundreds of innocent people, even as he bears the weight of ending the life of the one sent to kill many. But this same sniper could choose to use his skill to serve the terrorism movement. It is by his personal choice that he uses his ability to destroy many (by serving evil) or save many (by defending against evil).

So it is with the *ezer kenegdo*. God gives each woman the ability to choose if she will use her gifting from him to bring about what honors him and blesses her home. Every woman chooses. Every home is affected by her choice.

The first lines of this book gave us a picture of one *ezer* gone wrong. She was using her strength to get what she wanted. It was painful to witness, even for the ten seconds it was displayed. But oh the damage she was causing in her home.

When Wrong Turns Take Us to Unwanted Destinations

There are two predominant areas we will focus on in this chapter. Without a doubt, there are more ways an *ezer* can slide off the path God intended for her, but here we will look at some of the most common ways.

When writing this book, our inclination was to highlight the ways an *ezer* might use her warrior-like strength to dominate her home. Without a doubt, this is a huge problem in our world today— women who employ all kinds of tactics to get what they want. This we will call the controlling *ezer* (she must get her way). However, we want to be very careful to also note the subtler, but equally damaging way an *ezer* can veer off the path of God's good plans. The woman who overly submits and loses grasp of her own thoughts, abilities, personality, and call is over dominated by the demands of others and becomes the dreaded doormat wife.

It's like the wide swing of a great pendulum on an ancient grandfather clock. Some women swing far to the left as they work to submit, submit, and submit some more. They abdicate their role under the ruling authorities in their homes, losing their ability to stand up for what is good and right even if they know their homes are going down the dangerous path of destruction. The deep swing to the right of that pendulum is the woman who has had enough of other people telling her what she can and cannot do, and she is determined to have it her way, no matter the damage she inflicts on those around her. Neither of these extremes honors God, nor do they exhibit his intentions for the role of his daughters in their homes.

Before you get too frustrated (or even angry with me), let me confess something to you. I have been both of these women. It's one of the reasons you are reading this book. I began as the overly submissive wife. After several years of that not working out so well, I pushed back too hard and became the wife wanting to "take back" what I had lost. Both caused deep hurts. With all my heart, I was desperately trying to be a good person doing the right things. It saddens me to remember the angst of trying so hard and yet always knowing I was missing the mark. But God says he is able to use what was intended for harm to actually accomplish something good. This book is the telling of his willingness to do just that. We're exposing the ways I messed up and the ways we've seen others mess up, so you can know the truth and choose more wisely.

First, let's sit a while with the controlling *ezer*. She's working so hard to have it her way, but deep inside she knows something's not right.

The Overly Controlling Ezer

Please note: Husbands are just as capable of these offenses. These examples are not exclusive to wives. It is wrong to use any of these tactics in any relationship. But for the purposes of allowing an *ezer kenegdo* to recognize how easily her gift can be used wrongly, I have chosen to expose how it looks when the wife commits the offense.

Control

There are many kinds of control. In a marital relationship, control is when one is maintaining power or authority over the other. Too many husbands do this to their submissive wives. This is NOT what Jesus does with the church. Neither should it be what husbands do to their wives (love is not controlling).

However, too many women will use the warrior-like strength given to an *ezer kenegdo* wrongly as they work to control their husbands and their homes. This, too, is far from God's plan. A controlling attitude in a wife is like a hand made into a fist. It is not giving and generous of heart. It is demanding and forceful. This is at the root of many behaviors, each of which is working toward the same goal—getting her way.

This is the wife who smiled so sweetly and talked with a honey-coated voice in a conversation with us. Her husband stood beside her, quiet, smiling timidly. It was not that he was shy; it was that he was afraid to speak. She manipulated him with her sugarcoated words and he complied. But we knew her surface kindness had the potential to change the second we walked away if he didn't give her exactly what she wanted in our presence. She was a woman cat—able to purr sweetly one moment and draw quick blood with sharp claws the next. He lived in fear of her unpredictable ways. She was in control. Her *ezer kenegdo* call was denied in her home.

This is also the wife and mother who doesn't share with her husband the details of their household. The children will confide in her and she maintains control over who gets what and who goes where. She's the "just ask me if you need something, don't bother telling your dad because he's too busy anyway" mother. She knows her children will depend on her and not look to their father because she has trained them to do just that.

This man is most alone in his own home. He sees his family around him, but even sitting right beside them he knows somehow he is out of their circle of closeness. If he wants back "in," he will have to go through the mother.

This can happen intentionally or unintentionally. The husband can be so busy with work, hobbies, etc., that the wife takes on the full weight of caring for children, home, school events, doctor's appointments—everything. She sees it as her "job" to "help" the home. The father goes about his business. He thinks he needs to provide and not complain. The mother goes about her business. She thinks she needs to do all, be all, and control all concerning the children. Do you see how easily it can happen? Perhaps neither one of them is intentionally doing anything wrong. There is no mean-spiritedness. But let this dynamic continue for a few years and the children will grow up dependent on the mother, and the father will begin to wonder if he belongs there anymore. Can you hear the serpent hissing?

The mother has too much control (but it's possible she wasn't even trying to get it). The father has little (and he didn't even notice it slipping away). But in the end, Mom is in control. Dad is not, and aloneness has crept into the cracks. Control in the home can come wearing many different disguises, making it all the more difficult to uncover. Following are five common ways an *ezer*-gone-wrong can inflict much damage through control.

1. Manipulation

This is a tricky one, because it usually wears a mask like a high-stakes robber. Everyone knows something is being lost, but it's hard to say exactly what it is. When people are being manipulated, they are being influenced or persuaded—controlled.

But what does that r-e-a-l-l-y look like in a home? Well, believe it or not, it can come with a charming smile, a flirtatious glint in the eye, a special meal, or a candlelit dinner. But WAIT! Those can be good things, too, can't they? Absolutely. And it's our hope that every marriage enjoys these highlights... as long as they are the product of a sincere heart of love, LACKING manipulation. But manipulation will sometimes use this mask to cover its real intent. It takes what should be good and alters it, so that it is used to get what it wants.

The charming smile can be beguiling (enchanting, but used in a deceptive way). The flirtatious glint in the eye can appear to sparkle for the one it's looking at when, in fact, it is actually eagle-eye focused on something else it is trying to get—a new outfit, a new car, a new ring, a new… etc.

The special meal can turn from being a you-focused gift (for the husband) into a tool for persuading his thoughts. Distraction can aide a manipulator. A candlelit dinner can become a bargaining tool as the hope of what might come after the romantic dinner hangs precariously over the right responses during the dinner.

Manipulation can also come through the "please me or lose me" mask, but there's usually a sly grin under the mask. The manipulator doesn't actually want to be exposed. Instead, they are sneaky in quiet ways. She knows what she wants and she'll play the sweet game to get it. She is using her *ezer kenegdo* gifting for her own advantage. Perhaps she thinks she knows what is "best," and so rather than "work beside" her husband, she will "work him over" to have it. This wife leaves her husband feeling used and even deceived, because eventually he will realize the game being played in the relationship. Just as her manipulation wore a mask, so will his lack of trust.

Please understand that we're not saying candlelit, romantic dinners are traps of manipulation. We are using this one example to convey the reality that sometimes what SHOULD BE a wonderful experience can be used in wrong ways if the heart is not upright.

2. Demands

A demand is a pressing requirement. We can't ignore that this happens from husband to wife as well as wife to husband. It's a sure killer of relationships. It might not destroy the home right away, because someone will do his or her best to try and keep up with the demands of the other. But in the end, it is lethal to a couple's relationship.

For the purpose of this book, this marauding *ezer* is the wife who has a preset plan in her mind of how her life, her home, her marriage, her children, and her world will look. She oftentimes sees her husband as the delivery boy. She wants and he must get it for her or she will not be "happy." Her happiness hinges on his ability to meet her demands. The lady on the street at the beginning of this book is the picture of this. She will use her "strength" to require what she wants and oftentimes not even notice the poison she is pouring into her home.

This kind of *ezer*-gone-wrong is birthed in several ways. Maybe her parents spoiled her, surrendering to her every wish. She grew up thinking, I'm obviously supposed to have my way. Some might call this being spoiled. Others might call it self-indulgence. She's the wife who wakes up believing she knows what is best and will require it from whoever is available to deliver.

This type of thinking can gestate in the heart of a little girl who comes from roots of poverty as well. Growing up watching others having things she longs for can create a demanding attitude that will seek out ways to finally get what she never had before.

Both of these *ezer*s will use their *kenegdo* strength to be sure they have their way. Some women are focused on setting goals and reaching them. Applied correctly, this can be very beneficial. But the demanding wife slides off the good road by setting her own goals, making her own plans, and demanding that others follow her. She might feel good about her accomplishments, but her husband and those nearest her might silently wonder at her shiny selfishness. They know their dreams and goals are prioritized beneath hers, and their hurts are neither acknowledged nor cared for.

John 3:30 says, "He (Jesus) must become great, and I must become less." These words can transform the heart of a demanding wife if she will allow herself (and her wants and wishes) to decrease as she chooses to let Christ increase in her life.

3. Ultimatums

To give an ultimatum is to give a final demand or statement of terms, the rejection of which will result in retaliation or possibly even a breakdown of the relationship. There are times when it's appropriate to give ultimatums: to the employee not following company policy, to the child not obeying (not to lead to a breakdown of relationship, but for discipline/correction), to the homeowners refusing to make their monthly mortgage payments, and even to the spouse refusing to remain faithful or inflicting abuse in the home.

God does not require a spouse to endure abuse and/or adultery. If illegal or abusive activity is what the *ezer kenegdo* is working to stand against, and if she is using her strength to stand against an immoral wrong in her home, then she needs the support and prayerful help of the church around her. A great book that offers godly counsel in this type of situation is *The Emotionally Destructive Marriage* by Leslie Vernick.

However, barring abuse, adultery, and immoral or illegal activity by the husband, giving an ultimatum in order to have one's own way is wrong. The *ezer kenegdo* has gone awry when she gives her husband an ultimatum in order to get her way. This can be done subtly or overtly. Either way is woefully wrong and brings deep hurt to her husband.

When the words, "If you don't, then I'm going to" are spoken, ultimatums are being issued. The wife who demands she will not move away from her family even though her husband's job will require them to move, she is giving an ultimatum that does not honor God and will damage her home.

There are many sad stories concerning this kind of *ezer*-in-error damage. Here are two composite examples of what that might look like—two different homes. One survived. One didn't.

The husband loved his job and felt he was in line with God's will, but his wife became disenchanted with where they lived, so she demanded he find another job so they could move. If he did not comply, she would divorce him and take their children with her. After a period of struggle, he gave in to her demand. He could not bear the thought of losing his children. Their house remained intact, but their home suffered. Which parent do you believe the children viewed as the one in charge?

Yet another couple struggled in a similar way when he received a job transfer to another part of the country. The husband bore the full weight of providing for his family's needs; he had to work. His job paid very well, but to keep it, they would have to move. The wife sent him ahead to find a home and promised to follow him. He eagerly did his part, but sadly, after the new home was in order, she refused to join him. His heart broke as the home was divided. He was a trapped man. His desire to provide for his family left him living far from them, while his wife lived comfortably off his continued provision for their children. Eventually, divorce brought about the official breaking of their home, but everyone in the family knew the shattering began years before final papers were signed.

Ultimatums are ruthless ways to get one's way. An *ezer kenegdo* has been given strength and a warrior-like ability that if used in this wrong way will d-e-s-t-r-o-y the emotional heart of the man she should be standing beside. Rather than standing guard against the evil that would destroy her home, she opens the door to it. In both examples, homes were thrown off course because the headship of the home suffered a mutinous attack from the first mate, and all hands on deck tried to survive as the ship sailed through dark waters.

4. Expectations

An expectation is a strong belief that something should happen a certain way. This one can be easier to guard against, but it's very tricky in that it's difficult to recognize initially. Again, both spouses must be careful not to inflict this toxic behavior on the home. On every wedding day, the bride and groom gaze at each other with great hopes and hidden expectations. That is, unless they have received solid, Christian premarital mentoring.

These expectations begin forming in childhood. We either like the way our parents managed our homes or we don't. Based on our assessments of what we've seen, we will decide inwardly what will or will not happen in our homes. It can be little things or big things. Either has the potential to bring harm to the home.

Little things: who cleans the house, cooks the meals, takes out the trash, mows the grass

Big things: who pays the bills, manages the investments, keeps up with insurance needs

If the *ezer kenegdo* misuses her position as her husband's partner, she can begin to feel that she has a right to tell him what she "thinks" he should do. If he doesn't do it her way, she will say he's wrong. Every couple must take the time to determine what is "right" for their home to best function and bless all under its roof. An *ezer*-gone-wrong will refuse to realign her expectations and will instead require it to be done her way.

Good communication framed with respectful partnership will solve these problems of expectations. But left unmanaged, strong expectations will quickly misalign the home. God's Word reminds us of the good way: "This is what the Lord says: Be just and fair to all. Do what is right and good" (Isaiah 56:1).

5. Domination

When someone exercises power or influence over another person, he or she is working to dominate the relationship. We often think of husbands dominating wives, and, in truth, this does happen. However, there are a growing number of homes where wives are dominating their husbands.

This is very true in America, but it's also true throughout the world. Physical abuse of women is a worldwide problem. However, as more women have become educated and are equipped to hold positions of authority in society, the dynamic of dominance is being altered. Sadly, what had been used to dominate women is now being used by them as they push back against the centuries of oppression. Picture two people on a seesaw. When one is high, the other is low. But when the one on the low side pushes off, the high side comes down and the low side rises up to become the high side. The movement at the points of extreme is continual, while the middle of the seesaw never moves. It's the fulcrum point. It remains steady, no matter the movements at either end.

This is true in relational dominance as well. What once was high will in time (even though it take centuries) be brought low. And neither place is the place of balance and steady living. Thus it is with husbands and wives. If one is overly dominant, the other will eventually find a way to push off and rise too high, seeking to become the dominator.

Today, not only are some women dominating, some are becoming abusive. The daughter who grew up watching her father dominate and control her mother can grow into a woman who declares she will never be treated that way. To overcome, she may determine to become a dominator of her husband in an attempt to avoid being dominated. It's the seesaw effect played out in the home from one generation to another. But it must be corrected. How much better it would be to work together to reach a balance! The fulcrum strength is key; it should be our goal—the place in the middle where balance is found.

Dominance has been a problem since the garden. Some have accused Eve of dominating Adam. We don't agree. Eve did not make Adam taste the fruit. He chose to do so. However, their sons gave us the first real picture of domination when Cain murdered Abel because of jealousy. Cain could not bear Abel's offering to be more accepted than his own. So how did he dominate? He destroyed his brother.

We might not think of domination as a form of murder, but it is. When we want our own ways to the degree that we are willing to shut down the plans, hopes, and desires of others, we are dominating them. Emotionally, we are acting as if they are dead. Their wishes do not matter when compared to our own. This is domination—a form of emotional murder.

An *ezer kenegdo* who uses her warrior-like strength to maintain a power in her home and against her husband is bringing a type of death into her home. She will wonder why her husband shrinks away from her (emotionally), but his retreat will only empower her more. This is a home spiraling downward.

Domination is not right in the home by anyone. We should remember that God doesn't dominate us. He gives us the ability to choose. Christ doesn't dominate his church. We should never attempt to dominate one another. Scripture guides us to: "Do nothing out of selfish ambition or vain conceit. Rather, in humility value others above yourselves, not looking to your own interests but each of you to the interests of the others" (Philippians 2:3–4).

The Overly Submissive Ezer

On Her Knees
Several years ago, Steve and I met a family whose life story opened our eyes to the intense damage inflicted when a wife

becomes overly submissive. He was a minister, a pastor. She was a concert violinist. Together they had five children. They didn't own a home. Instead, they traveled from town to town in a very small motorhome, where some of their children slept on the floor since there were not enough beds.

Don't picture a luxurious, large camper. It was small and crowded, but it was what the husband said was "God's will" for their family. The wife shared with me one day that her family had strongly opposed their marriage. Her father had refused to agree to give his daughter's hand in marriage... saying he did not have a specific reason. In his heart, he knew she was not to marry this young man. He warned her that her life's dream of performing in beautiful concert halls before large audiences would most likely be lost if she chose to marry him.

But the young man was handsome and beguiling and he secretly continued pursuing her. In time, she rebuffed the warnings of her parents, snuck away in the night, and married him. Soon afterwards, the young man began using Scripture to control her. He warned her that she was not "cleaving" to him if she kept asking to visit her parents. She shared with me how she loved her parents and missed them terribly.

Eventually, the scolding she received from her husband exhausted her. She stopped asking to see them. They were not allowed to visit her. The husband stated that he was the head of their home and she was to submit to him or God would deal with her harshly. She never admitted it to me, but in her eyes she held a deep sorrow that implied there might have been times when her husband took it upon himself to deliver that harshness.

She lived in a small box with many children, an overly dominant husband, no connection to family, and no time to form friendships. Her lifelong love of music was her solace in the storm. She shared how she still practiced her beloved violin every day by putting a pillow under her knees in the camper and playing for hours when her husband was away and the children were doing schoolwork beside her.

She played her violin for us that day. Never have I heard an instrument cry as mournfully as her violin did resting on her shoulder. We were mesmerized by her ability to express her soul as the bow pressed down on thin strings.

I was young when I met her. I didn't know what I've learned since. But the picture of her playing her violin while kneeling on a pillow in a small, cramped camper has never left my mind. She had played in Carnegie Hall before marrying her husband. She was gifted with a talent that now only rang out in campgrounds. She lived in a box and was held there by Scripture used wrongly against her.

She truly believed she was pleasing God. Submitting to her husband was her supreme focus... never mind that her husband ignored the sorrow in her eyes and the longings of her heart. This beautiful woman had been deprived of her own thoughts and the pursuit of her God-given calling.

She was not a "balance" to her husband; she was his footstool. She was not a warrior in her home standing against evil. She was the cook, maid, child-bearer, and slave to a man who said he would be the only warrior in their home and if she thought otherwise, he would prove to her who was stronger. Once again, in his dark eyes, he used the Scripture that said she was weaker. He used the Bible as a hammer.

It has been years since we met this family. I have been told the man died several years ago. I don't know what became of the wife and her children. But how I hope they are happy somewhere, and I hope she has been able to enjoy life near her much-loved parents. She taught me something so valuable when I listened to her story. God never intended for a woman to be dominated and controlled by her husband. The submission a woman is directed to give to her husband is intended to be a gift to a man who is obeying God by loving his wife as Christ loves the church. There is no control. There is a cross. Submission is the woman's response in the dance of life beside a man who loves and protects her. Submission does not imply slavery. Submission speaks instead of a letting down of oneself in order to hear another and care for another in ways that reflect the love of God.

It Is To Be A Dance, Not Dominance

The Bible instructs a wife to submit to her husband. It is most clearly stated in Ephesians. There are three clear statements concerning submission:

> *Ephesians 5:22: "Wives, submit to your husbands as to the Lord."*

> *Ephesians 5:24b: "Wives should submit to their husbands in everything."*

> *Ephesians 5:33b: "The wife must respect her husband."*

In these same verses (Ephesians 5:22–33), there are four clear statements to the husbands concerning the call for them to love their wives:

> *Ephesians 5:25: "Husbands, love your wives just as Christ loved the church and gave himself up for her."*

> *Ephesians 28a: "Husbands ought to love their wives."*

> *Ephesians 28b: "He who loves his wife loves himself."*

> *Ephesians 33a: "However, each one of you also must love his wife as he loves himself."*

It is a dance that should happen between the husband and the wife. He moves with love; she moves with submission. She is safe to "let herself down" (the opposite of barricading herself from him). He advances toward her with love. She responds with a submission that speaks not of slavery but rather of loving care. They sway, each one doing the part given, and together it becomes a dance that inspires all who are near. Neither is controlling the other. Each is swaying with the other.

The invitation to dance is so often overlooked. It is found in Ephesians 5:21: "Submit to one another out of reverence for Christ." It's mutual submission that shows the goodness of the Savior's love in the middle of the home. Submission in the home is not about someone getting his or her own way. It's about someone needing to lead in the dance of love in the home. And the dance is not about one partner taking the spotlight. It should be about showing reverence for Christ. The dance of submission and love between a wife and her husband should leave us all breathless over the sight of Christ being loved between them.

The overly submissive wife is not dancing with her husband in this God-honoring way. She is being trampled by his dictatorship or control or manipulation. She is not dancing. She is trying to obey orders, or maybe she's just trying so hard to make him happy. She is not being loved as Christ loves the church (Ephesians 5:25), for Christ loved the church so much he gave himself up for it. The overly submissive wife might be intimidated into that position, as was the beautiful violinist. Sadly, there are some wives who actually make themselves less than God intended them to be. Why? Because someone, somewhere conveyed to them it was what they were supposed to do, and things went out of alignment as the good intentions of God were twisted and used wrongly.

Please keep in mind that we are trying to expose how something good (godly submission) can be twisted and used in destructive ways. It's so hard for this wounded wife to distinguish between God's way and her husband's way. She needs help to rightly understand the way her Father sees her and what his good intentions are for her.

One of the reasons we feel so passionately about the subject of submission is because we know just how easy it is to miss the mark and get it wrong. This was one of my downfalls in our early years of marriage. My dear Steve never asked (or wanted) me to be his doormat. But in my ignorance of what submission meant, I began placing myself in this position. I wanted to obey God, but I was overdoing it.

Steve didn't need me to disappear. He wanted and needed me to help him do life. He wanted a dance partner (and he doesn't even like to dance).

When preparing to write this book, a dear friend asked that I be sure and share the damage done when an *ezer* goes wrong by overly submitting. She shared her confusion growing up in her home where her mother gave all reverence to her father. Whatever the father said became the rule. The mother rarely, if ever, expressed her thoughts. Her energies were focused on how to best comply with whatever the father said. The girl grew up ridiculed by her father if she ever expressed an opinion contrary to his thinking. She was abandoned by her mother (emotionally) for not submitting to her father. It has taken her years to overcome the confusion this caused in her heart and mind. She loves both her parents dearly, but she did not grow up watching them "dance" with the symphony notes of love, respect, and mutual submission being played in their home.

How Can We Overcome the Tendency to Overly Submit?

If the husband is not demanding it, but instead the wife is going too far, then this aspect of *ezer* gone wrong can quickly begin changing. Four times Scripture refers to the lack of knowledge causing people to perish or die or be led astray: Job 36:12; Proverbs 5:23; Proverbs 10:21; and Hosea 4:6. So we are wise to seek truth and gain knowledge. The implication is that we will prosper if we will not remain ignorant. For this reason, we must gain a true understanding of the dance we are invited into within the beautiful symphony of marriage.

Love invites submission to dance. Love will lead; submission will respond. They move beautifully together, as each gives to the other, all out of reverence for Christ. "Submit yourselves one to another out of reverence for Christ" (Ephesians 5:21).

However, if the wife is being required to overly submit by a domineering husband, then good godly mentoring and/or counseling will likely be needed for a new understanding to come. Sometimes a new understanding can come just by reading books, which open the windows and let the light of truth shine in. We're flinging lots of windows open within these pages. We also highly recommend the book The Emotionally Destructive Marriage by Leslie Vernick. If possible, read it as a couple. If no one is dominating, then no one will mind reading it. But if a dominating husband is pressing his wife to be overly submissive, she should still read the book for her own growth and understanding and seek the help she will need.

We believe strongly that church leaders should read this book. The church has too long, perhaps unknowingly, promoted dominance while teaching submission. While teaching these truths in Kenya, we have had prominent pastors wipe tears from their eyes as they confessed the harm that had come to many women who had been told by the church they should "try harder" and be more submissive. Many of these women were then beaten to death or burned alive or slashed to death or incurred deadly diseases from their unfaithful, overly dominant, submission-demanding husbands. The stories are nightmarish, but they are true. And these tearful pastors confess these stories are from church-going homes.

These are stories of overly submissive women trying their best to "obey God" and follow the guidance of church leaders. But their overly submissive posture took them to places that were never the intention of the One who made them.

Do you believe this happens all over the world?

Is it possible this is happening in your country, your neighborhood, and your church? Perhaps not in the extremes mentioned above, but in more quiet, subtle ways? Or is it possible the biblical command for wives to submit to their husbands is being used to silence wives from asking for the help her home needs?

"Be just and fair to all. Do what is right and good."

We hope you will revisit this chapter from time to time for the purpose of self- examination. We too often get so busy with the activities and demands of daily life that we lose the ability to honestly see ourselves. May the exposing of these commonly missed, but relationally toxic, practices be used to open our eyes and compel us to change what needs to change so that *ezer kenegdo*s can bless our homes and no longer be hindered.

Chapter 9

Did it end with Eve?

Birds, bees, and butterflies all look to the dandelion for their survival. Dandelions are an important source of nectar and pollen early in the season for bees. They are food plants for the larvae of butterflies, and birds rely on the consistent seed production as their food. Without the perseverance of the quiet, unpretentious dandelion flower, much beauty would be lost.

For the Sake of Her Husband

Her sleep was tormented. She tossed and turned. She had had dreams before, but never like this one. The roar of the crowd outside their palatial home matched the noise inside her head. The courts of the praetorium vibrated with lies that day, but what could she do? She had heard the rumblings against this man Jesus, but she knew little of him. Her tormented night was now reflected in the angry shouts of the crowd and standing before them was this one silent man.

False accusations were hurled at him, but he said not a word. She knew he was innocent. Did her husband? With all the pressures that came down on Pilate's shoulders, was it possible for him to look past the angry crowd and know the truth? The visitor in her dreams had been clear—this man was innocent. If her husband, Pilate, executed Jesus, innocent blood would smear Pilate's hands. And she knew deep inside that this blood mattered more than any before. Was she to remain silent in her pampered world of plenty? *She couldn't.* She cared deeply for her husband and, strangely, she cared for this Jesus. She lived in a world ruled by men, some who even thought they were gods. Dare she speak? Would her husband hear her?

Quickly, she grabbed writing reed and ink, taking a small piece of papyrus paper, she wrote, "Leave that innocent man alone. I suffered through a terrible nightmare about him last night" (Matthew 27:19).

The servant delivered the note to Pilate, the governor, who sat quite uncomfortably before Jesus. Pilate was no fool. He realized the leading priests had arrested Jesus out of envy (Mark 15:10). Pilate knew. The words *ezer kenegdo* would have never crossed their lips. Those ancient Hebrew words had remained tucked away in the garden. But beside him, Pilate had been given the gift of one. Her name was Claudia.

She was not trying to gain power, not seeking attention. She was not looking for personal gain. Instead, her heart and soul were for what was right for both her husband and the man in front of him— Jesus. She had been given an insight, a knowing. It had come to her in a dream.

An *ezer kenegdo* will have the courage to speak what should be spoken in ways that are beneficial for all.

A lesser woman might fold into herself and just look for comfort after a sleepless night. Not Claudia. But just because an *ezer* speaks does not mean she will be heard. Sadly, Pilate succumbed to the pressure of the religious leaders and ranting crowds. Jesus, under Pilate's watch, was flogged, handed over to the crowd, and crucified.

We know nothing of Pilate's personal thoughts regarding the outcome of that day. But according to historical records, Pilate made sure Jesus was buried. It was by his command that guards were placed at the tomb. Later, Pilate wrote that Jesus was crucified, recording it in his official ledgers, which were sent to Rome to be archived. There could be no question that Jesus had been killed by crucifixion; his death was recorded in Roman history, thereby proving his resurrection was also factual by the testimony of Roman guards at the tomb (Matthew 28:4).

Did Pilate and Claudia privately discuss her dream, the note, or his ruling? Only they know. Greek historians would later record that under the rule of Emperor Caligula, Pilate committed suicide. It is believed by many that prior to his death, both Pilate and Claudia accepted Christ as their personal Savior.

Claudia has been the focus of many books and poems, all stemming from less than 40 words found in one verse, a verse that does not even give her name. Why? It's the beauty of an *ezer kenegdo* who appeared briefly, not even by name, not even showing her face in the praetorium that day, but surely doing the work of the Father as she attempted to bring a right influence to her husband. The fact that Pilate ignored her warning doesn't fall on her shoulders. It rests on his. Instead, for all of history, Claudia is remembered as the woman who tried to stand for what was right in her home. And she did so with the grace and poise of a true *ezer*.

She's not alone. There are many women in the ancient pages of the Bible who lived out their namesake—those words whispered over them by the Creator. God is himself an *ezer*, a helper, to those who call on him. He breathes his *ezer*ness into his daughters. Imagine how he desires for his girls to know it and live it and bless those around them with it.

For the Sake of a Child

During the same days Claudia lived, there walked a woman who loved Jesus more than any other. But she was likely not present in the courts of Pilate that day. The mother of Jesus, Mary, was an *ezer kenegdo* if ever one lived. She was the young lady engaged to Joseph, a descendant of King David. The angel Gabriel visited her when she was possibly as young as 13. Some historians believe she was about 14 years old when she gave birth to Jesus. (This is based on Jewish practices 2,000 years ago.)

While her young age astounds us, let's not forget that an angel visited her and brought her a message from God. And he called her "blessed among women, favored." Gabriel told Mary: "The Lord is with you" (Luke 1:28)! Perhaps you are so familiar with the story that you miss the fine-line beauty of this young *ezer kenegdo*.

The very next verse in Luke shares about Mary's honesty and humility. She was confused as she tried to understand what the angel was saying. She wouldn't try to be perfect. She was allowed to be herself. And the angel responded to her humanity by saying the most beautiful words: "Don't be afraid Mary, for you have found favor with God!" (v. 30). There was, without a doubt, a beautiful *ezer*ness about Mary. God knew she would not carelessly raise his Son. Instead, she would grow him up well—protect, nurture, guide, and foster in him the strength that comes from an obedient, willing *ezer kenegdo*. Even as Gabriel was sharing with Mary all that was about to happen, the angel pointed her in the direction of another *ezer kenegdo*, her cousin Elizabeth, who was also carrying a child. God loves for his *ezer* daughters to support one another.

The Word tells us that a few days after Gabriel's visit, Mary hurried away to the hill country of Judea to the town where Elizabeth lived. And recorded for us is the support and encouragement these two women gave to each other, even to the degree that the child Elizabeth carried (John the Baptist) leapt inside her when she heard Mary's voice. Both of these *ezer*s were being called to raise powerful men that would change the world. Elizabeth said these words to young Mary: "You are blessed because you believed that the Lord would do what he said" (Luke 1:45).

Mary stayed with Elizabeth about three months and then returned to her parents. Imagine the courage she needed to face her parents, Joseph, and the village, none of which knew of her pregnancy. She was strong. She was willing to stand for what she knew to be right. She was a young *ezer kenegdo*.

Elizabeth, too, was a woman willing to live out her *ezer* calling from God. Luke 1, beginning with verse 5, tells us the story of Elizabeth and Zechariah. They were highly respected in the eyes of the community and righteous in the eyes of God (v. 6). They were careful to obey the Lord and had done so for many years. The Scripture says they were both very old. They too received a visit from Gabriel (six months before he visited Mary). Gabriel spoke to Zechariah, giving him careful instructions, but Zechariah showed doubt and pressed his questions too hard.

Gabriel stilled his tongue, making him mute. Shortly afterwards, Elizabeth became pregnant and was thrilled that the Lord had chosen to show her such kindness in her old age. For the entire pregnancy, Zechariah remained unable to speak. After Mary's three-month visit, and upon her return home, Elizabeth gave birth to the son Gabriel had told Zechariah would come—a son who was to be named John, who would be filled with the Holy Spirit at birth. He would turn many to the Lord and would prepare the way for the coming of the Lord (vs.15–17).

The community gathered around them for the naming of the boy. The people wanted to name him Zechariah after his father. But the *ezer kenegdo* in Elizabeth showed when she boldly said, "No! His name is John" (v. 60)! Those around her were shocked. How could she not name their only son after his father? They asked Zechariah what he wanted to name his son. And with a writing tablet, he wrote, "His name is John" (vs. 62–63). At that moment, Zechariah regained his ability to speak (v. 64).

It's necessary to look at the complete story for the purpose of seeing the shining *ezer* moment when Elizabeth honored both God and her husband. Elizabeth had the courage to stand firmly against the pressures of the community around her. In doing so, she was standing with her husband, Zechariah. Gabriel had instructed him as to the name the child should receive. Elizabeth was supporting those instructions even with the frustration it caused those around her. She was strong. She was an *ezer kenegdo* called on to raise John the Baptist. God searched and found a woman willing to live her *ezer* calling. He knew she would pour that strength, obedience, and warrior-like support into this boy who would grow into a man, who would baptize Jesus and boldly declare his arrival.

God sees the woman who is willing to live out her namesake. He does amazing things through her.

Some think, Well, of course, Mary, the mother of Jesus, was a strong lady, but how hard could it be to raise a God-child? Although Jesus was the Son of God and was sinless, he was still a child who needed to be raised right. He faced all the things children face. He had needs. And perhaps Mary's *ezer*ness showed up most profoundly in the way she was able to withstand the glares of those around her through her pregnancy, delivery, and mothering of this child. Joseph, too, was a remarkable man to obey the angel (Matthew 1:20–21) and go against customs and traditions. If he had followed those customs, according to Jewish law, Mary would have been stoned for becoming pregnant outside of marriage. What a beautiful couple they had to have been in God's eyes... Joseph willing to embrace the *ezer* God gave him, Mary willing to live out her calling. Mary, Elizabeth, and Claudia lived in the days of Christ. But let's travel back to the Old Testament and visit another *ezer*.

For the Sake of Her Home

In the book of 1 Samuel, we find the story of a woman who is perhaps one of the most exquisite examples of an *ezer kenegdo* in her day. Saul was still king, but jealousy had enraged him against David, who had already been anointed by Samuel to be the future king. As Saul and his army chased David and his men, the kingdom of Israel hung precariously in the hands of an unstable king. It was about 1000 BC.

The power of Egypt had declined; the Chou dynasty in China was in full swing; and the Mayan dynasties in Central America had just begun. But in the wilderness of Paran, near the town of Carmel, lived Nabal and his wife, Abigail. Nabal was a crude, mean man, but he was wealthy in land and livestock. His wife, Abigail, was a sensible woman who managed his household well. But he was not appreciative of her good qualities. Instead, he focused on his success and his enjoyment of his wealth. 1 Samuel 25 tells their story. It's worth grabbing your Bible and reading.

While running from King Saul, David and his men were hiding near Carmel. Nabal's shepherds grazed their flocks nearby, but had no problems with David's men. Not one sheep or goat went missing even though David's men were often hungry. One day David heard that Nabal was shearing his sheep, so he sent men to ask Nabal if he would share something to eat with David's men. David knew Nabal had more than enough to share and he hoped he would be generous.

Nabal did not reply favorably. Instead, he ranted at the messengers and sent them away empty-handed. When David heard of Nabal's words, his anger raged, and with 400 men, he rode intending to deliver his response in person. They would destroy Nabal and all of his household.

But a servant went to Abigail and told her all that had happened. The servant explained, *"These men of David's were very good to us... more than just good. They offered protection for both our flocks and all of us when we neared their camp. But now, our master has brought great trouble on us all. None of us can talk to him because of his ill temper, but we are in great danger because of the way he has spoken to David's men."*

After listening to the servant's warning, Abigail acted quickly. She gathered food and drink, loaded it on donkeys, and traveled to intersect the men she knew would be coming to destroy her home. Abigail did not tell Nabal what she was doing. She knew what needed to happen, and she would do it alone.

As Abigail saw David and his men coming in the distance, she quickly got off her donkey and bowed low. When David came near, she shared with him that she knew her husband, Nabal, was a wicked, ill-tempered, foolish man. She asked David to accept her apology for the way Nabal had acted and to receive all the food she had brought to them as a gift. She spoke blessings over David asking that he not take vengeance.

David responded to Abigail's apology by accepting her gifts and telling her to return home in peace. But even more, David publicly thanked God for Abigail's good sense, because her actions kept him from killing many that day.

She saved the lives of everyone in her home—family and servants alike. She was an *ezer kenegdo* who knew she was not able to balance the wrongs of her husband, but still she stood firmly for what was right. Her *ezer*-ness saved her home. But that's not the end of the story.

When Abigail returned home, she found a drunk Nabal throwing a party, celebrating the harvesting of wool from the sheep. She didn't tell him what had happened. She knew a drunk man could hear nothing. But the next morning, when Nabal was sober, Abigail told him all that had happened. Nabal had a stroke right there before her eyes. For nine days he lay paralyzed. On the tenth day, he died. The Bible says, "The Lord struck him, and he died" (1 Samuel 25:38).

Nabal's wrongs were between the Lord and him. And the Lord dealt with Nabal. But Nabal's death was not on the hands of Abigail. She did nothing to harm him. Instead, she did all she could to bless and help him.

That too is a quality of an *ezer kenegdo*.

Even married to a harsh, ill-tempered man, Abigail remained faithful to the *ezer* calling inside her. She chose the good ways, even when her husband chose the wrong ways. And she didn't let Nabal's ugliness alter her beauty and wisdom. She stood alone beside her foolish husband. She didn't agree with him, support him, or act like him. She was honest with David about the kind of man Nabal was. But she remained faithful to her household and did all she could to protect and bless it.

Abigail's is a story of an *ezer kenegdo* who is overlooked and unappreciated. But her story does not end with Nabal's death. Instead, shortly after, David sent messengers to Abigail asking her to become his wife. David saw the value of Abigail's *ezer*-ness.

We can find more *ezer*s in the Bible: Queen Esther, Hannah, Deborah, Sarah, and Ruth. There are many whose names are never given. They were the quiet, busy, strong ones who stood bravely for what was right and fought against evil—the unknown *ezer*s who protected their homes, encouraged many, remained faithful, and honored God.

Those two lost, hidden Hebrew words spoken by God in Genesis might not have made it out of the garden, but the call to be God's *ezer* daughters can be heard throughout history. They're the women who have carried his purposes with the strength of warriors willing to stand beside their husbands to accomplish what is good and right. They are still there, making a powerful difference.

Did it end with Eve?

Chapter 10

Reclaiming that Moment in the Garden

The dandelion blooms its perfect yellow circle, and then within 9–15 days, it closes its petals, grows long in stem, and finally opens again into the puffy, ripe seed head commonly called a puffball.

The Father's Heart Toward the Ezers He Created

A layover in Amsterdam left us wondering what to do with eight extra hours. Having never been there before, we boarded a train and headed to the historic city. Locks control the waterways. Old buildings hold history in their aging cracks. Winding streets carry you to tree-lined walkways and street cafes.

We saw her when we paused to take a picture of the beautiful street with flower boxes and blooming trees. It was perfect weather, crisp air and blue skies. The day sparkled. As Steve stood posing beside a tree, and I raised the camera to capture all that I could, there she was sitting in the large window. She was alone, completely alone. Bits of flesh were covered by sparse pieces of silk. She sat on a metal stool. I lowered my camera and our eyes met. I'd never heard of Amsterdam's Red Light District; naivety can land you in unexpected places. There was no long stare or unkind exchange between us. She was about my daughter's age, and my heart passed through the large glass window to her. She knew she was not being judged. She was being seen, not as an object, but as a girl.

Some might criticize me for these next words, but from my heart, I believe the One who made her loves her still. No garment changes that. No window seat alters his love. No rudeness or crudeness of choices changes the great LOVE of the Father. His love overpowers our wrongs. He loved us all so much that "He sent his one and only Son, that whosoever believed in him would not perish but have eternal life. God sent his Son into the world not to judge the world, but to save the world through him" (John 3:16–17).

The One who made the young woman in the window loves her. And HE made her to be an *ezer kenegdo* (her choices do not alter his purpose). It's breathed into every woman he creates. But in this world, troubles come, serpents spout deadly words, and so many flounder in the wake of rough waters.

Do you believe someone can "perish" and yet still be loved by God? Just ask the mother and father who have done all they can to help their son who is addicted to drugs. Do they love him deeply, even as they watch him fall?

It's true for every daughter (and son too).

The One who made her breathed into her a purpose to be an ezer kenegdo in a world filled with trouble.

To rise up to that call, she will need to understand it.

To understand it, she must be taught the truth behind it.

To be taught that truth, someone must care enough about her to share it with her.

And she should know it will not be easy. It will require the help of the One who made her.

Nothing Easy About It

There are many challenges to living as an *ezer kenegdo*. Just because we learn the truth doesn't make it easy to begin living that way.

Isn't it probable that the disciples of Jesus felt the same way? If we remember rightly, the bridge between learning all Jesus taught them and living what he said, found them huddled in an upper room behind closed doors. They were frightened at the prospect of living out his call on their lives without him leading them in person. They'd just seen him crucified and laid in a tomb. Their courage was smothered under the weight of the stone that sealed that tomb.

The young woman in the window's courage was being smothered under the weight of not knowing the One who loved her completely. When I looked at her, I remembered the story of another woman long ago—the immoral woman who brought a beautiful alabaster jar filled with expensive perfume. She knelt behind Jesus, wept, and pouring the perfume on his dusty feet, wiped them with her own hair. She was criticized by the Pharisee, but not by Jesus. Grab your Bible and read it for yourself (Luke 7:36–50).

Let yourself really picture that moment. The air was rich with her gift of extravagance. She knew she wasn't worthy, but her focus was not on her worthiness. She was riveted on HIS goodness. She was willing to endure the skeptical eyes of others in order to love the One who is good. She was rejected by others... but not by him. And what did the Son of God do? He saw her; he loved her; he received her gift. And he said of her, "I tell you, her sins—and they are many— have been forgiven as she has shown me much love. But a person who is forgiven little shows only little love."

This woman was willing to reach for the ezer kenegdo hope she saw in the eyes of Jesus.

If the enemy of God, the cunning serpent, the liar that feeds poisonous thoughts, if he can make us believe we are unseen, unloved, and unworthy, then he can destroy the truth. The fruit of deception will be eaten again and again and again, and the good plans of our Father can be missed just as often. Please hang close with me in these last two chapters. It's one of the most crucial wallowings we need to sit with.

The Lie Is Closer Than We Think

The young woman in the window where red lights glow at night has believed a lie. She somehow thinks that's all she can do, that's all there is for her. She has been treated so wrongly, she's not able to see herself the way the One who loves her still sees her. I was raised in a home with beautiful parents who did all they could to give me every good chance in this world. They protected me, cared for me, introduced me to God, and loved me. But a little girl growing up in an almost perfect place still gets lied to. It's not just the immoral woman or the warped mind or the street child or the serial killer. Even a loved daughter safely tucked into crisp, clean sheets with a full stomach is vulnerable to the serpent's hiss.

When I was a little girl, I was mischievous and playful in childlike ways. I woke up happy (usually) and stayed that way all day (usually). But, if or when I misbehaved and was caught, I had figured out a way to avoid discipline. Somehow from an early age I was skilled at telling bold-faced lies. After it worked a few times, I quickly adopted it as a game. Whether I needed to lie or not, sometimes I just would. How many times could I lie before getting caught? How much could I get away with? And while it entertained me for a time, in the end it bit me harder than a starving lion. How?

Every Sunday, my parents took us to church, and there I began to understand that we could hide nothing from God. That meant that even though I had gotten away with tricking my parents, I could not trick God. He saw everything, and HE KNEW I was a liar. It horrified me. I was ashamed of who I was and I was only 11 years old.

I looked at other kids and thought, You're so much better than me. I'm the worst kind of person in the world. It had only taken one decade for the destroyer to find a slithering way into my head, even in my parents carefully guarded home.

Then during a summer revival, the preacher got to me. It was a fear-filled sermon for sure. He said, "If you die tonight without confessing your sins and asking Jesus to become your Savior, then you will spend eternity in hell." I understood eternity meant... f-o-r-e-v-e-r.

I looked at my dad and knew he couldn't save me.
I looked at my mom and knew she couldn't help me.
I looked at my sister and brother and knew they were witnesses to what a liar I was.
The gig was up.

So with wobbling knees, I walked the 100 miles from the back of the church to the front, where the screaming preacher stood. I prayed exactly what he told me to pray. Then he looked at me and asked, "Now, don't you feel better?"

I was determined that for the first time in a long time, I was not going to lie. After all, God would know if I tried to, and he would surely strike me dead on the spot if I lied to the preacher. So I shook my head no. I didn't feel better. He prayed again. I copied his words. Was I better yet? No. Again, he prayed. Again, I tried. No.

Couldn't the preacher see what was happening? At 11 years old, I was too bad. God wouldn't let me in. I was the worst kid in the world. I wondered how long it would take for everyone to see that I could not be saved.

Then a hand rested on my shoulder and a woman's voice said, "Will you come with me? I have something to share with you." I couldn't get up fast enough. She was giving me a way out. At least when God's rejection came, I wouldn't be at the front of the church.

She walked me to a small room. With the kindest of smiles, she opened her Bible and laid it between us. She asked me what was wrong. I shared the truth with her. No lying allowed; this was too important. I told her how I was the worst kid in the world and God knew it. He knew what a liar I was, and even though he forgave other people, there was no way he could forgive me. I'd messed up too much. And she did the most amazing thing. She asked me to read a verse from her Bible. I could do that. I could read. God might not want me, but I could read.

She turned to different verses and asked me to read them. I did. Then she said, "Now, we're going to read all these verses again, but we are going to change the words a bit. Can you do that?" "Yes."

She explained that every time the Bible verse used the words "the world" or "Israel" or "my," then I should substitute my name. Sounded like a game to my 11-year-old mind. I nodded my head okay.

We read through Psalm 23, and it sounded like this:
The Lord is Donna's shepherd; she shall not be in want. He makes Donna lie down in green pastures; He leads Donna beside still waters. He restores Donna's soul...

John 3:16 became:
For God so loved Donna that He sent His one and only son, that if Donna would believe on His name she would not perish, but she would have everlasting life.

Luke 7:47 became:
I tell you, Donna's sins—and they are many—have been forgiven. So Donna will show much love. A person who is forgiven little shows only little love (and my little 11-year- old mind saw some hope).

So, I thought, *God, does this really mean that the number of sins doesn't matter to you? It's the amount of love I'll show that matters? And I'll be able to show more love because I've been flooded by your love for me? I could live to love and not die in lies?*

I asked this preacher's wife, and she smiled with a warrior strength, looked deeply into my eyes, and said, "You will love better because his love will cover those wrongs inside you, and the more spaces he has to cover, the more places his love will be."

I never knew her name.

But I remember her ezer presence in front of me. She taught me to let the truth in the Bible move into me, to let God change me through his truth. His truth trumps every lie. God wins.

She prayed Scripture prayers over me, putting my name in God's Word, and I felt grace for the first time in my little life. I didn't know what it was, but I felt it move in.

The Truth Is Closer Still

Personalizing the Scriptures, like I did when I was 11, is a very helpful way to better understand the truth of Scripture in your life. In addition, praying Scripture by inserting your name or another's name is beneficial. However, we must always remember to return to the original text for deeper study, reflection, and application. It's the original text that is profitable for teaching, reproof, correction and training in righteousness (2 Timothy 3:16).

For the girl behind the glass window, her sins were many. Her eyes said it. But did she know about the lady who poured the perfume on Jesus' feet? Did she know that where lots of sin is found, there's the chance, in God's hands, for lots of love to flow? If she could know, then she could begin to see that even she was created to be an *ezer kenegdo*.

The little liar who walked the church aisle was certain she was the worst person who had ever lived. That little girl didn't even know there were red-light streets or women on stools behind glass windows. If she had, she would have still thought she was worse than them. It was the plan of the serpent to bring her down and destroy her future.

There are millions of ways we daughters of God are tricked. The goal of the serpent was to destroy the relationship between God and his image-bearers, Adam and Eve, as well as their relationship with each other. The sequence of events... the serpent's arrival in the garden reveals that he knew he needed to stop this *ezer kenegdo*, as God had called her. Otherwise, she might prove to be too strong of an ally for the man. And he's been working to stop *ezer kenegdo*s since.

If he can stop them behind a window where red lights shine at night, *he will*. If he can stop them when they're little girls, *he will*. If he can encourage their feelings of insufficiency and insecurity, *he will*. If he can stop them from believing they were created by God to be *ezer kenegdo*s, *he will*. If he can stop them by discouraging them in their marriages, *he will*. If he can stop them by convincing them it's too late, *he will*. He doesn't come as a serpent in a garden today. Instead, he comes as a thought, an impression, or a doubt. But when he comes, it is to destroy.

The Truth Is for All (No One Is Left Out)

For the *ezer kenegdo* who feels like the young woman in the window waiting for red lights to glow, please read the story in Luke of the woman who poured perfume on Jesus' feet.

For the little girl (even if she's all grown up now and looks like a woman) who believes she's too bad, she's sinned too much, she's too far gone, and there's no way God would even consider accepting her now, please read my testimony again. I didn't make it up, and don't believe for a second that what happened to an 11-year-old girl doesn't apply to a woman full-grown. That would be a lie. And remember, I know a lie when I see one. Please "sit" with that precious, nameless preacher's wife. Hold her hand and let's read those holy words with YOUR name in them. It's the one truth you can know is for you.

For the woman who feels so unable, insufficient, unseen, and insecure, please remember that the heart of God toward you is not reflected in the hearts of those around you that have caused you to feel so weak and frightened. God's heart whispers to his girls the essence of warrior strength standing against evil—standing for what is good and honorable and upright and true. All else are lies. For the woman who still doubts those Hebrew words were even spoken by the Creator, please research it yourself. If I found it, you can too. Remember his words, *"Ask and it will be given to you; seek and you will find; knock and the door will be opened to you" (Matthew 7:7).*

For the woman who struggles in her marriage (silently or loudly), who wrestles with submission, who feels dominated by an overbearing husband, or who recognizes she's been using her strengths in wrong ways, please carry it in prayer to God and ask for his help. I had to.

We all need help. Not one of us is perfect; not one of us is without error. Go back and reread the parts of this book that spoke to your heart. Face what has been wrong; ask for forgiveness (from God, yes, but perhaps from others if you've wounded them in your struggling). And let God begin his good work of restoration and remodeling inside you.

Just as the preacher's wife prayed Scripture over me, you can begin doing this as well.

Chapter 11

Planting for a Harvest

The flower blooms closer to the ground, sometimes only an inch high, while the puffball raises its head high, up to eight inches tall, so the wind (or a child) can blow it far. Each petal of the flower produces one seed for the wind to carry. Dandelion seeds have been known to travel up to five miles on the wind.

Praying It

As I was writing this book, God overwhelmed me one morning during my time alone with him. I came upon Isaiah 62:1–5 and was so touched by the sincerity of the prophet's prayer over the city of Jerusalem. His love for that city and the people living there was a mirror reflection of God's love for them. And it struck me that if a man could pray over a city in this way, shouldn't an *ezer kenegdo* be willing to pray over her husband just as fervently? After all, the love any wife has for her husband is meant to be a reflection of God's love for him. So I tried it. I put Steve's name in the appropriate places. Rather than pray for a city, as Isaiah did, I could pray for my man instead. So I did. And suddenly I was overwhelmed by the same sensation I had with the preacher's wife as she put my name into the Holy words. What a beautiful way for an *ezer kenegdo* to be a warrior against evil and beside her husband.

I hope you'll give this gift to your husband as well. You don't have to tell him, but you might want to. And it might help him to begin seeing you as an *ezer-kenegdo* daughter of God. Just put your husband's name in the blanks. It's a perfect way to "pull your sword" (Ephesians 6:17) and stand *ezer-kenegdo* style in your home.

> *Isaiah 62:1–5*
> *"Because I love God, I will not keep still. Because my heart yearns for _____, I cannot remain silent. I will not stop praying for him until his righteousness shines like the dawn, and his salvation blazes like a burning torch. Others will*

see his righteousness and leaders will be blinded by the glory of God in him. And _____ will be given a new name by the Lord's own mouth. The Lord will hold _____ in his hand for all to see—a splendid crown in the hand of God. Never again will _____ be called [   ] or [   ]. (In these two spaces list two things about your husband you pray will be taken away (e.g., stubbornness, selfishness, pride, laziness, arrogance, weakness, fearfulness, being a taskmaster, being a workaholic.)

His new name will be [   ] and [   ]. (In these two spaces, list two things you want God to grow in your husband. Be sure these are God-honoring attributes that will bless your home and not just self-serving qualities (humility, generosity, kindness, faithfulness, wisdom, etc.).

For the Lord delights in _____ and will claim _____ as a part of his bride. Our children will commit themselves to the Lord, please God, just as a young man commits himself to his bride. Then God will rejoice over _____ as a bridegroom rejoices over his bride. Oh, Lord, post watchmen on our walls; and have them pray day and night. And I will take no rest as I pray to you, Lord, just as I will give you no rest until your work is complete."

The Choice Is Yours

Regardless of how others might view the call to live as the *ezer kenegdo*s we were born to be, each woman must first understand it fully (oh, how I hope this book has helped you there) and then make her own decision regarding her willingness to live out this calling.

Up until the sharing of this garden secret, in many ways the awareness of a choice was hidden, at least for many of us. Now, however, I hope it is much clearer and the newly found purpose is a very real option. We have a new chance to choose a way we might never have realized was even an option. And if we'll be brave enough to do so, we'll find tucked inside us the God-given ability to be a new kind of helper, one who brings balance in the home and can rise like a warrior to protect those in our care. What a gift! What a responsibility. What an exciting, life-giving way to live.

Time Waits for No One

2 Corinthians 5:10: "For we must all appear before the judgment seat of Christ, so that each of us may receive what is due us for the things done while in the body, whether good or bad."

One of the ways I measure myself, my choices, my actions, or my lack thereof is by imagining the moment before God 2 Corinthians 5:10 speaks about: *"For we must all appear before the judgment seat."* It's not a fear-based imagining. I do not believe God is just waiting for the chance to punish me. Rather, it's a love-based imagining, because I know he is a good Father who is hoping I will have followed his ways. I believe God wants to celebrate with us. It's why he prepares a home for us (John 14:13).

But before that time comes, there are things God wants... things he hopes for. And believe it or not, he waits to see if we are willing to care more for his heart than our own. Don't misunderstand; I'm not saying God "needs" anything from us. Only that in his great heart, he hopes for good to come through us. This good will come from him and flow through to others. But, in the meantime, it will renew us. Imagine it—God is willing to patiently wait for us to choose him, even though he chose us long ago. So often we wring our hands, pray, and hope God will give us what we want. But do we ever stop to think about the fact that he, too, is hoping. He *hopes* we will hear the desires of his heart! He doesn't force us to follow his way, but he knows if we will, good will come—for us, yes, but also for those around us. It puts wind in my sails to see it this way. Rather than me waiting (sometimes with heels dug in and arms crossed in a huff) for God to give me what I want, why don't I consider all he has already done for me, all he has already given? Grace upon grace is the way John wrote it in John 1:16. Imagine how things might change if we lean more in the direction of becoming what he created us to be.

Think of the difference it could make for those living beside us. If we will live out the *ezer kenegdo* call he put in us, oh what a difference it will make both now, during our breathing days, as well as then, when no more earth air is needed. It's a very sobering thought, but one that should recalibrate us.

Does it feel like I'm overdoing it here? I am.

If I were standing beside you on a busy street corner, and just as you stepped out into the street, I saw a car coming that you had not seen, wouldn't you want me to pull you back? (If it were me about to step in front of a car, please stop me.)

What if each time you went to cross the street, more cars came? Would you want me to continue reaching for you, or would you think I was overdoing it? Hopefully, you'd feel the love in the persistence of my reach.

It's because this matters so much that I keep pressing. It matters for your home now, but it's possible that on the day we breathe our last breaths and step into eternity, it might matter most. Rather than wait until then to think about all we could have done, why not weigh it out carefully now and live it fully from this day forward?

Living out your *ezer kenegdo* calling is not a salvation issue. If you have accepted Christ as your Savior, then his gift of salvation is yours. What hangs in the balance is whether you will have lived your life with the fullness of the call God breathed into you.

I love how Paul says it in Colossians 1:22: *"Yet now he has reconciled you to himself through the death of Christ in his physical body. As a result, he has brought you into his own presence, and you are holy and blameless as you stand before him without a single fault (NLT).*

When you stand before your Father in the moments after your life here is done, it's not condemnation or criticism you will face. If you choose him as your Father and accept Christ's gift at the cross, Paul says that God sees you as holy and blameless, without a single fault. (That's all because of Christ in you.) So whether or not you live out your *ezer kenegdo* call, your salvation will not be impacted. Instead, it will impact your personal knowing, your realization, your everything-is-clear-now moment before God. You'll know if you missed the *ezer* mark or not. It won't change God's love for you. But you will know if you missed what could have been and settled for less, when God had intended so much more good for your home, your marriage, and your relationships.

Choose carefully. You won't get to do the days over again. So love well, speak carefully, pause to think, listen more, make it count, stand like a warrior against evil, bring balance, protect your home—love well.

Recently, Steve and I were camping near Mt. Kenya. The sun had set, baboons had filled the tree on the horizon, and animal sounds shifted from daytime calls to nighttime noises as we sat around our campfire. Hearing something strange in the distance, I shined a light into the darkness. I couldn't believe my eyes. In the distance, a good 100 yards from us, was the low-crouching approach of a lion, his wild mane shifting on his shoulders with each step as he advanced toward our camp. Now you would think I would have screamed and run to the truck. Most people probably would have. Instead, I took a step forward, asking Steve, "Is that really what I think it is? Is that really a lio------?" And before I could get the word out of my mouth, Steve was grabbing my shoulders, pulling me toward the truck, saying, "Yes, it's a lion. Get in the truck now!"

Who knew two 50-somethings could move so fast?

It shocked even me that I had lingered at what I was seeing. But as we sat in the truck, peering out fogged-up windows, I realized that my mind had been so conditioned to being able to watch a replay of an exciting moment on television, that here in real life I was expecting to see a slow-motion replay to confirm what I was seeing. Even typing this now, I'm amazed at the way my mind was programmed to have a "second look." It's true, isn't it? We are used to having another look, perhaps another chance to see more clearly.

But in real life, there are no instant-replay moments. You can't run the tape back and have another look... "in slow motion this time, please."

There will be a moment that will be your last.

After that, you won't be able to say one... more... word. So, it's imperative that you live it out well, knowing why you're breathing and seeing the approaching lion for what it really is.

If you feel like an Abigail, trying to live like an *ezer kenegdo* beside someone who makes bad choices, remember this: she did not allow Nabal's bad choices to drag her down into his pit. She still lived out her calling. On her day of standing before the throne at the end of her life, she won't have to give excuses for her choices concerning Nabal based on what Nabal had or had not done. Nabal's choices were his, and her choices were hers, and they each stood separately before God. Abigail won't be saying, "If he hadn't, then I wouldn't have..." Instead, she will be saying, "I did what I was supposed to do, regardless of what he chose to do."

When I was young, it was ridiculous how often I would base my decisions on what my friends were doing. I remember thinking if we got into trouble, then at least I wouldn't be alone. They say misery loves company. Well, I must have figured punishment was less painful if someone was sharing it with me.

Then as I grew older, I came to see how true it was... that hard times faced alone are so much worse than faced with someone nearby.

Is it possible we look at that great throne moment in the same way? Do we wonder if we have to look again at a wrong choice, we'll be able to endure the correction with our fingers pointed at those who were a part of our choices, saying, "I only acted that way because she . . ."? After all, sometimes it worked with our parents, right?

It's just that we won't be able to point our fingers or pull anyone else into our moment. Our choices will be ours, and no one else's choices will be allowed to weigh in on our moments after earth and before eternity.

It's an unpleasant thought, yes, but one that wisdom asks us to have a long, honest look at.

On the night the lion was approaching our campsite, I would have been foolish to keep watching his approach. For within the minute, he might have ended my life and there would have been no more chances to go back and do it a better way.

It's a raw finality in life. When it's over... it's over. None of us will get a do-over. So shouldn't we give it all we've got for the one round we do get?

Psalm 90:12 (KJV): *"So teach us to number our days, that we may apply our hearts unto wisdom."*

It's just a hunch, but I believe those first moments of looking into the face of Love, a transformation at a glance will happen. We'll know more in that moment than we've learned in a lifetime.

And what will we be thinking... if we can think?

We might want to say, "Give me another chance, Lord, now that I completely realize your amazing love for me, now that I see it was always about you and your love and never about me and my wants. Let me have a do-over Lord, and this time I'll be the *ezer kenegdo* you created me to be."

To be clear here, God will not **love you** more or less based on whether you did or did not live out your call. No, he loves you completely already.

What is on the line is whether you will have lived your life to its fullest with an inner peace that can only come from knowing you ran your own personal *ezer kenegdo* "race" all the way to the finish line. There's a peace that is found in that solid place of understanding and living the call.

So we must choose carefully how we live today, because there will come a tomorrow that will be our last. It's what "numbering our days" means—taking a long look at how we are living the days we are given and choosing to apply the choices we make so that wisdom guides our hearts. .

A last word from Steve:
Men, we have a responsibility too.

If you are a man reading this, or if your wife is reading it to you, I urge you to listen. Listen with a large dose of humility to hear beyond the voice of pride that would try to influence you to tune out the message. It is not your spouse speaking, although in her heart she may be hoping you will begin to understand the call God intended for a woman. She may be trying to understand the depth of what it really means to be an *ezer kenegdo*. **And you have the responsibility to help her get to that place.**

For decades, men and women have been missing the point of position for the woman due in part to the definition of one word—"helper." Serving as missionaries in Kenya and being saturated in the language of Kiswahili, we find many times that what the people are trying to communicate to us in their language doesn't transfer with the same effect as it is intended. Much gets lost in the translation. The meaning becomes "watered down" and loses its full impact. The same has happened when the name *ezer* **became "helper." As it has been mentioned many times in this book, God refers to himself as an** *ezer*, **"a help in time of trouble" (Psalm 46:1). That certainly strengthens the meaning of "helper," causing me to pay attention.**

This past Christmas, Donna bought me a First-Century Study Bible. The descriptive subtitle reads: "Explore Scripture In Its Jewish and Early Christian Context."

So original Hebrew words are explained throughout the book, painting a better picture of how it really was in biblical days. When I read Genesis 2:18, this Bible's version (NIV) still reads, "helper suitable," but the footnotes brought some new insight:

There is not a single other ancient source that contains a story of woman's creation. And here, six verses are given to the creation of woman as opposed to one verse for the creation of man. The Bible clearly elevates the woman, making her the completion of creation itself. The term "helper" (Hebrew 'ezer) in verse 18 is not demeaning; the same word is used to describe God's relationship to humanity. Using a wordplay for 'ezer in Hebrew, the rabbis claimed that woman's intelligence surpasses man's." (NIV First-Century Study Bible, Zondervan, 2014, pg. 8, with notes by Kent Dobson)

Since God was the one who gave women this title, who are we to question?

Who are we to downgrade the role of a woman, her status, her position, her place beside us, or her place in the world? How foolish to overlook the intimate details of our Creator's appointed role of the woman. His purpose in making her was to make you complete. He created her for you! God equipped women to watch your back when you can't see the whole picture. If you are married, think about the times your wife has tried to help you see something that wasn't apparent. When you were about to make a financial miscalculation and she was the one who pointed out the blunder, did you listen? Did you listen or were you too prideful to hear her? I have made that mistake too many times. It was not God's intention for us to do it all or to know it all. He knew the difficulties in this life would require the two, acting as one, to work together to solve problems.

Several years ago, I sat for a week with an elderly gentleman, a wise man that helped me better understand my position as husband. He said, "Son, you can't do this alone. That is why God gave you a wife and she sounds like a good one. Go home. Listen to her. Hear her opinions and ideas. Show her respect. Give God that respect. Ephesians 5:21 says, "Submit yourselves, one to another out of reverence for Christ.' Not everything she says will be right, but you owe it to her to listen. Then, you take that information to God before making decisions. God sometimes speaks to you through your wife."

And so I began listening and hearing the more God had for us both. It has changed our home for the original good he intended for us both.

When we married, Donna and I were both believers in Christ and working to do what was right in the eyes of God. In our best efforts, we fell short. Well, I fell a bit shorter than she did, but we both wanted the same thing and that was to please God and live our lives for him. We are not uncommon. You may feel the same way, wondering why your marriage is not working out the way it does in the movies.

Well, you don't live in the movies. Life is real and it doesn't take an attorney or a theologian to figure it out. Most marriages struggle for the same reasons. In the game of football, the players are given a playbook of the strategies they will execute on the field. The military devises plans for war. Corporations have guidelines for the success of their businesses. Your board games come with instructions on how to play.

Just like these examples, we were given a playbook to guide us through life in obedience to the One who created us. Isaiah 48:18 says:

"If only you had paid attention to my commands, your peace would have been like a river. Your righteousness like the waves of the sea."

When we began to wonder why our marriage wasn't turning out like the ones in the movies, Donna started digging for answers. Then I joined the search. Together, we could see that we weren't fully following God's instruction book. Today, we work to be more obedient. Don't misunderstand. We haven't discovered life's secrets, but the path we are on is bringing freedom and joy into our home. That's why we're sharing it with you, not as a reprimand, but as an encouragement for your marriage and your life in general. This book has been written out of the same obedience—as a gift to you. We hope it has helped you find some treasure that was left in the Garden long ago. It's our prayer for you.

From the Heart of the King

That moment in the garden, with bone in hand, all this and more rolled through the heart of the Creator. He knew their days would be numbered. He knew man alone was not good. He knew this ezer kenegdo would be the perfect solution to the aloneness. He knew the serpent was coming and the man would need a warrior beside him. God knew they would need to work together, not to elevate one and diminish the other. No, they would each need the other to choose God's ways for the good of the home he would give them. But even more than that, he knew this soul-carrying, image-bearing daughter of his would hold and nurture every person he would create from that day to this. Her work would be more than she might realize, but, oh, the good plans he put into place when he breathed life into her!

He looked down at the first daughter as he formed her in his hands. It was a private moment, just the Creator and his girl. And in his greatness, he knew she would be like him in ways that would please him immensely. He hoped she would choose to let him accomplish his good plans in her, for her, and through her. He would name her after himself. She would be his gift to man. He called her ezer kenegdo.

THE END

The *Kiss*

A kiss of affirmation came the day after the initial writing of this book was completed. Steve announced we should celebrate by taking a nice long hike in a park near our home in Kenya.

We packed a picnic and grabbed our hiking shoes. Sharing the trails with elands, zebras, warthogs, and impalas, we enjoyed every minute of the day. Then we returned to our car and headed home.

Driving slowly out the dusty road, we encountered a young couple walking. The man motioned, asking for a lift. Steve said, "I know we don't normally do this, but something tells me we should give them a ride. What do you say?" "Sure," I responded.

We quickly said a prayer asking for protection and pulled to the side of the road. They were a young couple on their honeymoon touring Kenya together. Strong accents let us know they were not "from these parts," as we'd have said back home in Georgia.

Conversation flowed easily after introductions were shared. They were from Israel, had been married one month, and were fluent in many languages. Their preferred language and mother tongue was Hebrew.

Now, allow me to pause to say that for years I have been reading and studying all I could concerning the two Hebrew words "ezer kenegdo," but neither Steve nor I had been able to find a solid pronunciation. This had troubled me greatly since I wasn't sure I could accurately share what I was writing about if I couldn't correctly pronounce it.

I began asking how to pronounce different English words in Hebrew. They were so gracious, giving careful language translation lessons. Then I asked if they happened to know of the two words God had used in the book of Genesis when he was speaking of the gift he would give to Adam to solve the problem of his aloneness. I offered my poor pronunciation but had not even gotten the e-z-e-r out of my mouth when the young bride said (with her wonderful accent), "You mean ezer kenegdo, the name God gave to the first woman, his first daughter?"

And there it was, pronounced beautifully. After months of searching, God had delivered it to us. I said, "Yes. Oh how we've wanted to hear those words spoken accurately!" I took out my phone and they both kindly repeated the words several times so I could record them. There they were, spoken exactly as Moses or Abraham or GOD would have said them. It felt sort of . . . holy.

I briefly shared that I had just finished writing a book about ezer kenegdo, explaining that in English translations the two words usually come out simply as a "helper suitable." She said, "Oh, yes, I've heard this. But it is so sad, because ezer kenegdo means so much more than those words suggest."

Holy filled the air even more. I said, "You are right. Would you tell me what you believe the two Hebrew words mean?" As Steve is my witness, this dear young woman (whose name was Eve!) began saying much of what I'd spent pages trying to explain. She knew. She confirmed. And then she said, "I'm so thankful to hear you've written it in a book for all the world to read. I would not know of it myself if my mother had not been careful to teach me. People need to know what God intended when he created that first woman. It's important, but somehow it was buried in the garden on the day the serpent came." From the mouth of a beautiful bride from Israel, God confirmed to us his heart's desire for the words to no longer be buried. Doubt was defeated. You now hold his gift in your hands.

I pressed an inch further and asked one last question. Wanting to know if the ever-present dandelion flower grew in the land where that first perfect garden held those first uttered words, and if perhaps Jesus may have paused to pick one on the side of the dusty trails he traversed, I asked if they knew of the little flower that grew wild, had hundreds of yellow petals forming a perfect circle, called a dandelion? Questioning faces responded. Steve took out his phone and pulled up an image of the flower. Bright smiles came when they said, "Yes! We call it a taraxacum flower and they grow everywhere in our homeland."

Conversation was sweet as they confirmed that without a doubt, Jesus would have seen this little weed-flower and likely bent to pick them often since, when needed, it is also taken as food. And perhaps, dare we even say probably, this tiny flower even grew in that first perfect garden, where the words you now know were first uttered.

It is Steve's and my prayer for you that this book has given you new treasure and maybe even a changed heart. May you see dandelion flowers everywhere you go, and may they remind you of the heart the Father still has for his princess daughters.

Acknowledgements

Who knew writing a book would require so much help? There are many fingerprints on this offering, it feels somehow wrong to have my name alone listed as the author. It takes a group of like-minded hearts to come up with a worthwhile finished product. This book has been through many think-tanks and passed across many computer screens. So where do I begin?

I'm so thankful to the many authors who have written snippets here and there so my searching eyes could find answers. Stasi Eldredge and Carolyn Custis James you're at the top of my list. Thank you for writing. I thank the many ladies in my life who have lived out their ezer kenegdo calling. You are proof to me, that God wants his daughters to carry his purposes still today. I've watched many of you from a distance, some of you from up-close; you rarely knew I sat in a desk in the classroom of your life. Oh I thank God for you!

Thank you Dawn Hurley for bringing your expertise to my efforts.

It was inspiring to watch how you could sharpen the point and trim away excess. Without your help, I would have given up.

Thank you Jess Cozzens for being the first to read through the rough-rough draft and offering your professional eye for detail and give important suggestions. One whole chapter was birthed from our conversations; important things I would have missed. You are a gift in this world.

Thank you Paul Cox for your careful guidance over meticulous details. You were willing to hear the heart of the message in the words while making sure the message stayed grounded in good theology. Thank you for loving God and his Word, and for being our friend.

Thank you Maggie Taylor Lian for your creative professional touch to the cover design and page layout. One of the things that kept me up at night, was an unquenchable longing to write all this for you --- and for all the little girls still to come. I wanted you, the ezer kenegdo I gave birth to, to know the truth of what the One who made you sees in you. Spoken words can too easily be forgotten. Written words can go much further. As you've designed the creative details of this book, my joy has overflowed knowing you'd finally be able to hold these treasured truths in your hands. May the words ezer kenegdo come alive again in the generations ahead of us dear.

Thank you to my closest friends for your encouragements to w-r-i-t-e... Does anyone ever really think themselves able to put into words what is needed? You girls know how I've struggled with stringing letters into words to fill the places where aching spaces hide. I've had big spaces inside me where echoing winds blew ------ but you girlfriends knew what to do. Caverns stop echoing when you fill them. Thank you dear ones for continuing to be friends who bring good --- always.

Dear Steve, how can I thank you enough for your steadfast reminder that my writing is just another way to worship the One who is my everything. Abba creates and gives ---- and invites us to join in. You've pressed me when I wanted to quit trying, encouraged me when I doubted, called me out when I feared what people might think, and reminded me of what Jesus could do with fishermen who were willing. You and I both know our marriage is far from perfect --- and we still fall down sometimes. But our imperfections fit perfectly in the hands of the Perfect One, and he's not done with us yet. Thank you Steve for loving God, and for loving me. I'm blessed in the flow of you and God together.

And where do I find those right words to thank the One, the KING, my Shepherd, our Abba. How thankful I am that he knows my heart and hears what words are unable to say. He hears every word spoken in laughter, every syllable sound in a moan. Thank you God for being willing to let your goodness travel in clay vessels. Thank you for taking bone-in-hand and breathing your life into us. Ten thousand thank yous --- is only the beginning...and I know they likely don't read books in Heaven... but just in case... i'd like to call ahead and reserve a coffee-date with Ruth Bell Graham, Corrie Ten Boom, Mother Teresa, and my sweet grandmother... I want to thank them for so much.

May we always remember,
Donna

Questions for Reflection
and Discussion

Chapter 1

1. Why have women rarely heard the words ezer kenegdo? Why has the world (and even the church) missed these treasured words causing women to lose sight of their God-given calling?

2. Do you view the word "helper" (when referring a wife) as a demotion in the home? Why or why not? How do you think the world/other cultures views the word "helper" (when referring to women)?

3. Why are most women not able to see themselves as God's beautiful ezer kenegdos?

Chapter 2

1. What new revelations have you received while reading about the timing of the serpents arrival? His conversation with Eve? Adams presence and "absence" in that first serpent encounter?

2. When we see the pain of others, we can be stirred immensely. What causes us to sometimes miss the pain in our own lives? Our own relationships? In the lives of those closest to us?

3. When we hear of injustices committed in far away places, do we care or do we respond internally with a numbness? What

would "caring" entail? If we sense a distancing and numbness, what might be the antidote that wakes us up?

4. Pray and ask God to open your eyes to see the ways the "garden attack" is still going on today. What are some ways you see it still impacting today's relationships?

Chapter 3

1. Learning that the Hebrew word ezer means "helper" and "support and aid as found in military strategies and victories"; have you ever witnessed an ezer-ness in a woman in your life that was misunderstood? If she (and those around her) had understood this quality, would it have made a difference? If so, how?

2. Has this chapter helped you see that an ezer is still an ezer whether she is married or not? How do you see the qualities of an ezer even though she may not be married? What might hinder this?

3. Imagine if soldiers on a battlefield spent more time comparing themselves to each other than focusing on their enemy. They would not be able to win that battle. Discuss the many ways ezer kenegdos are so often distracted and ineffective under the shadow of comparison.

Chapter 4

1. How have you previously defined the words, "helper suitable"? What thoughts arise when you read that, ezer could mean something like lifesaver? Contrast the two?

2. "Roles change with the wind. Identities should not." Discuss how this concrete understanding can benefit the ezer kenegdo and those who live with her.

3. It has been said that the greatest challenge adolescents and young adults face is their confusion over and/or loss of identity, they're wondering who they really are in the face of peer-pressure and social media. Do you agree?

4. How do you think it might help girls and young women if they could understand the meaning of the words ezer kenegdo? How might it help boys and young men?

Chapter 5

1. What emotions and thoughts do the following words evoke: "Since the first ezer kenegdo failed in the garden of Eden, all ezer kenegdos will fail."?

2. Many cultures and countries oppress women, some even using the story of Eve in the Bible against women today. Do you believe it is to the advantage of the "serpent" (the devil) to keep women oppressed? If no, then why do you think it happens? If yes, what can be done to change hearts and minds so ezer kenegdos can be seen for who they are meant to be?

3. Reflect on these words from this chapter, "They will work to apply each of their abilities in ways that will complement the other's abilities. Therefore, they accomplish a greater strength unified than either of them would have had alone." Do you believe

marriages today (yours or others) reflect this strength of unity? If yes, what encouraged this to happen? If no, how can they begin moving from where they are to where they could be?

Chapter 6

1. What does it mean to the the head of the home? (If reading this as a couple or in a small group setting, be sure all have a chance to respond.)

2. What does it mean to be a submissive wife? (Again, listen to different perspectives.)

3. Are you willing to accept the role of the ezer as a warrior who will stand against anything trying to cause harm to her home? If no, why? If yes, discuss examples of how her warrior-like way might look.

4. How do you think others will view the warrior-like behaviors of an ezer kenegdo?

5. How do ways of an ezer support the headship of her husband?

Chapter 7

1. Before reading this chapter, how would you have explained "the two will become one flesh" (Mark 10:8)?

2. Have you ever considered "spiritual intimacy" as form of closeness in marriage?

3. Do you think physical intimacy or spiritual intimacy has the greater potential for carrying a couple through hard times? Explain your answer.

4. If you are married, on a scale of 1–10, where do you believe your spiritual intimacy is with your spouse (1 being very weak, 10 being very high)? Discuss with your spouse and consider making a plan to increase your "two becoming one" spiritual intimacy level. (Ideas: read a book together to enhance your walk with God and each other, pray together, leave prayer notes for one another, plan a quarterly getaway to enjoy each other's company and pray together for your home.

5. Consider writing your own personal mission statement. Here's a rough draft you can edit and fill in:
"I, _____, would someday hope to be remembered as a person of _____
_____. I believe God made me for a good purpose. Knowing my spouse, children, and grandchildren will be impacted by my choices, I will show my love for them by _____
_____
_____.

Chapter 8

1. Do I dominate others in my home in order to get what I want? If so, how?

2. Do I know what my husband/wife, children, or future spouse hopes for, dreams of?

3. Have those in my home been drained of their ability to hope and dream because of trying to keep up with my demands?

4. Have I manipulated others to get my own way?

5. If married, did we agree with each other about expectations we brought into our marriage? Or did we just bump into each other until one of us won? Do I need to apologize? Do I need to forgive?

Chapter 9

1. Is there another ezer kenegdo story in the Bible? Who is she? What aspect of ezer-ness does her example show?

2. Explain the common threads of ezer-ness that connect these very different ladies living in very different places.

3. Ezers will look to other ezers for mentoring and support. How can this help them accomplish their individual callings?

4. Will ezers be well liked by those around them?

5. Does wealth or affluence limit the ezer? Does poverty? Why do you think so?

Chapter 10

1. Do you believe the One who made you loves you no matter what you've done?

If not, why? Can you trace backwards to find the thing that kept you from seeing His love?

If yes, are you living in response to that love? Do you let others feel its flow? Daily?

2. An ezer kenegdo is willing to go it alone if she needs to, like the preacher's wife who had the courage to invite me into the Holy Words. I later learned she was criticized by some for having done that. It wasn't the "normal" way --- how thankful I am she was willing to risk criticism for the sake of a little girl. Can you think of an ezer kenegdo woman in your life who has made a difference? Who was she? If she's still living? Would you be willing to thank her? Would you please introduce her to the words – ezer kenegdo?

3. Please accept an invitation into the Holy Words? Read Psalms 23 replacing the my's and me's with your name. Please read it out loud. And if you happen to be reading this with others, would you please read it to one another inserting each other's names? It's a good, new, right way to see yourself and those beside you.

Chapter 11

1. In what ways would it change your choices/actions/thoughts today if you lived each day with your focus set on the words that might be spoken when it's all over and you stand before God?

Does that thought frighten you or inspire you? If neither, then what feeling does it evoke in you? How do you think God might view that conversation? Do you believe love will be present?

2. If you have made choices that discourage you when you think of that moment, what can you do now to change the course of the conversation to come? Forgive someone? Ask for forgiveness? Have a conversation? Pray for someone?

3. If you are a woman, are you willing to begin living out your ezer-kenegdo calling? If so, what 3 changes are you willing to make today to begin? Share them with someone, write them down, pray and ask God to help you, each morning plan ahead for ways you can help your home and those in it by being God's ezer.

If you are a man, are you willing to support the women in your life (wife, friend, sister, daughter) to understand and live out the purpose God created them for? Do you understand it will take courage for her to try? How can you help her?

Made in the USA
Columbia, SC
02 December 2017